HOW TO CLIMB™ SERIES

Conditioning for Climbers

The Complete Exercise Guide

Eric J. Hörst

FALCONGUIDES ®

GUILFORD, CONNECTICUT
HELENA, MONTANA

AN IMPRINT OF THE GLOBE PEQUOT PRESS

FALCONGUIDES®

Text design by Casey Shain
Interior photos by Eric J. Hörst, unless otherwise credited
Charts and tables by Casey Shain, Lori Enik, and Mary Ballachino

Library of Congress Cataloging-in-Publication Data
Hörst, Eric J.
   Conditioning for climbers: the complete exercise guide/Eric J. Hörst.
     —1st ed.
     p. cm.—(How to climb series) (FalconGuides)
   Includes index.
   ISBN: 978-0-7627-4228-8
1. Rock climbing—Training. 2. Exercise. I. Title.
   GV200.2.H66 2008
   796.522'3—dc22

2007029314

Conditioning for Climbers

*To my original training partner
and life hero, Jeff Batzer.*

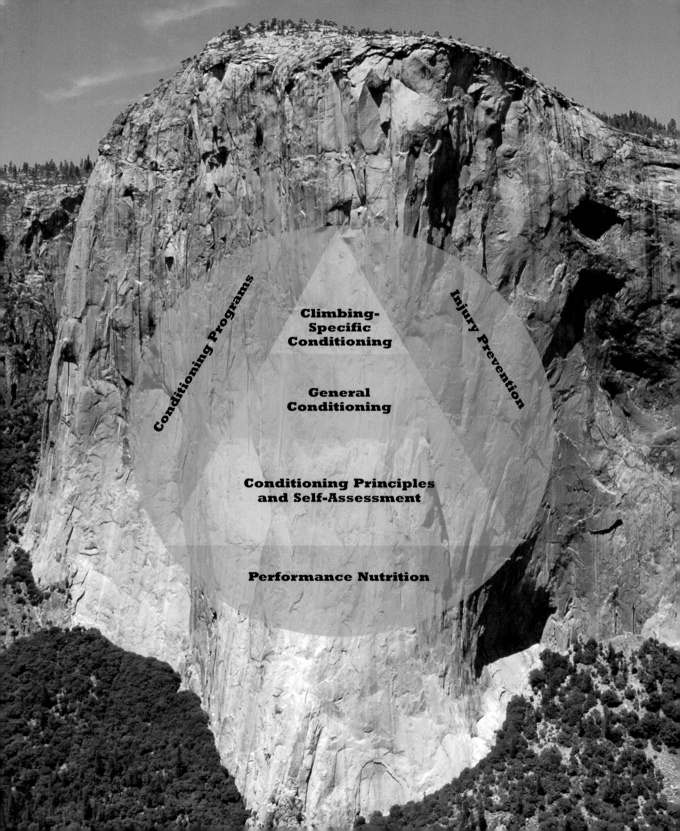

Climbing-
Specific
Conditioning

Conditioning Programs

Injury Prevention

General
Conditioning

Conditioning Principles
and Self-Assessment

Performance Nutrition

CONTENTS

ACKNOWLEDGMENTS

The idea for *Conditioning for Climbers* came from the many climbers who urged me to write a book focusing solely on physical conditioning. Given the wealth of positive feedback on my previous books, I decided to accept this challenge and spend a year exercising my fingers on a keyboard. I hope that I meet or exceed the expectations of these climbers, and I thank all of those folks who have encouraged me.

My deepest gratitude goes out to all the climbers I have worked with or talked training with over the years, whether in person, by phone, or over the Internet. It's this interaction that inspires and energizes me to spend frequent late nights and weekends writing climbing books, at the expense of many a good night's sleep and the occasional missed weekend of climbing. Similarly, I am grateful for the climbing companies that continue to support—and enhance—my endeavors both on the rock and as a performance coach and author. Foremost I must thank Nate and Pam Postma, Greg, Kimberly, and everyone else at Nicros, Inc. You guys are such a big part of my various training projects, and I tremendously enjoy working with you all! Likewise, I thank Colin, Jonathan, and Stephanie at La Sportiva for keeping me climbing in the best shoes on the planet. Ditto to Carolyn, Jim, and Paul at Sterling Ropes for supplying my lifelines, and to Christian Griffith for the stylish threads that appear in many photos throughout this book.

The process of creating this book begins and ends with all the good folks at FalconGuides and The Globe Pequot Press. Many thanks to Jeff Serena, Scott Adams, Shelley Wolf, Casey Shain, and everyone who unbeknownst to me has helped enhance this book in some way. And what would this book be without the many beautiful instructional photos? Shooting these photos was a major production for me, and I appreciate everyone who contributed both in front of and behind the camera. Thanks to Eric McCallister, Randy Levensaler, Matt Calardo, Nikki Baillie, Laura Mae Hornberger, Josh DeGeorges, Jessica Rohm, Keith McCallister, Mark Himelfarb, Crystal Norman, and L.A. for lending your talents to this project. Many thanks also to Earth Treks and Cliffhangers for allowing me to shoot instructional photos on your great climbing walls!

Above all I am thankful for my wife, Lisa Ann, for her unconditional love, support, and understanding of the long hours it takes to write these climbing books. I similarly cherish the understanding and inspiration afforded to me by my sons, Cameron and Jonathan—I truly value our time together above all else! And to my parents: I am blessed to have you in my life and still following my climbing after more than three decades.

Veteran hardman and La Sportiva USA president, Colin Lantz, bouldering in the Front Range of Colorado.

PHOTO BY STEWART GREEN,
COURTESY HÖRST COLLECTION

INTRODUCTION

Conditioning for climbing is as different from other sports' training programs as vertical departs from horizontal.

Since you are holding this book in your hands, I trust that you already know firsthand that climbing is a rigorous physical sport that will test your strength, power, endurance, flexibility, and stamina. Elevating climbing performance therefore demands that you enhance your conditioning in each of these areas, as well as elevating your technical and mental skills. While there are numerous books available that touch on these subjects, there has been no comprehensive exercise book for climbers—until now.

Conditioning for Climbers is the ultimate manual for climbers who are looking to improve their physical capabilities. Regardless of your age, ability, or sports background, this book will empower you to develop and engage in a supremely effective conditioning program. And as you progress as a climber, *Conditioning for Climbers* will guide you in modifying your program for long-term benefits that will keep you upwardly mobile for many years to come.

Without a doubt, piecing together an optimal exercise program for *you* is like solving a complex and completely unique puzzle. The fact is that the vast majority of climbers do not train optimally—in fact, some of the workouts I've observed over the years arguably provide no benefit on the rock! I have therefore written *Conditioning for Climbers* to guide you through all the essential steps of effective conditioning, from self-assessment to program design to proper execution of the exercises. All the while I have tried to avoid going unnecessarily deeply into exercise science or describing esoteric

training practices, with the goal of crafting a streamlined, content-rich book filled with practical how-to information. The bottom line: There is no more complete instruction available short of me working with you one-on-one as your personal performance coach.

Conditioning for Climbers is divided into four parts containing twelve chapters. Part 1 provides an overview of the core principles of effective conditioning, as well as the most detailed self-assessment worksheet ever devised for climbers. Accurate self-assessment is an essential precursor to developing a conditioning program that will really work for you. Like a prism, this forty-question assessment will separate out all the areas that influence your climbing performance, thus revealing your true limiting constraints and empowering you to target them with training.

Parts 2 and 3 provide the most complete array of conditioning-for-climbers exercises ever assembled in a single book. Chapters 3, 4, and 5 cover all aspects of general conditioning, including warm-up and flexibility exercises, entry-level strength training and weight-loss tips, and fifteen fabulous core-conditioning exercises. Chapters 6 through 9 then delve into the rich area of climbing-specific exercises. You will learn more than twenty effective exercises to target the all-important muscles of the fingers, arms, and upper torso, with strategies for developing strength, power, and endurance. Though overlooked in most other books, you will also find an entire chapter on training the antagonistic muscle groups that are so vital for maintaining muscle balance and reducing injury risk. Rounding out the instruction is a chapter on stamina conditioning to increase your capacity to climb long days and excel in high-altitude settings.

In the final section, part 4, you will learn how to assemble a comprehensive training program that

PHOTO BY ERIC J. HÖRST

xiii

works. Based on the results of your self-assessment, chapter 10 will guide you in selecting and combining exercises from throughout the book to make up your weekly conditioning program. Workout schedules are provided for beginner, intermediate, and advanced ability levels, so this book will remain your companion for effective training as you climb your way up the grading scale! In chapter 11 you will find what I hope will be enlightening and inspiring information on optimal conditioning for youth, women, and over-fifty climbers—three groups that I view as especially gifted at climbing. Chapter 12 then wraps things up with coverage of a few of my favorite subjects—ironically topics overlooked by many climbers—including the power of performance nutrition, the benefits of periodization and planned breaks from climbing, and the secrets to avoiding injury.

As you read *Conditioning for Climbers,* you may occasionally come upon unfamiliar muscle groups, scientific terms, or climbing lingo. Flip to the back of the book for a glossary of terms and anatomy photos showing all major muscle groups.

Before we dive into the exciting subject of conditioning for climbing, I must stress once more that excellence in climbing is more than muscle and might. While increasing your physical capabilities is absolutely essential, so is developing superlative technique and mental skills. Vow to work constantly on all three aspects of the climbing performance triad—physical, mental, and technical—and I guarantee that you will perform beyond your expectations and succeed in reaching your goals and beyond. Now let's get conditioning!

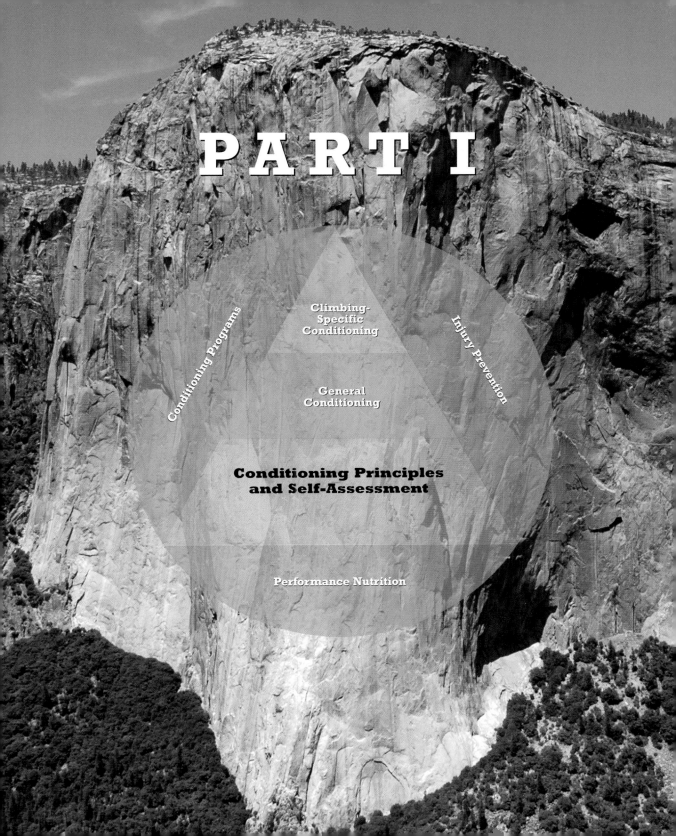

PART I

Conditioning Programs

Climbing-
Specific
Conditioning

Injury Prevention

General
Conditioning

**Conditioning Principles
and Self-Assessment**

Performance Nutrition

Principles for Effective Conditioning

The key to excellent results is not training harder, but training smarter. Premeditating your workouts and acting in accordance with the principles of effective training are the essence of smart training.

Conditioning for climbing is as different from other sports' training programs as vertical departs from horizontal. No matter your previous sports experience, you can probably forget much of what you learned about physical conditioning. Consider that it is leg strength and power that generally matter most in field and court sports, while exceptional cardiovascular conditioning and stamina are required for endurance sports such as running and biking. By contrast, the physical constraints of rock climbing relate mostly to arm and finger strength, upper-body power, and a high level of anaerobic endurance. Consequently, getting in shape for climbing requires a highly distinct conditioning program.

Conditioning for many traditional sports involves weight training to build strength and mass, which in turn yields more force and inertia for engaging the opponent. In climbing, however, you might view gravity as the lone opponent, with excessive body mass and lumbering, inefficient

Climber on American Sportsman (5.10c), Red Rocks, Nevada. PHOTO BY ERIC J. HÖRST

movement playing to her favor. Therefore, a climber's conditioning program should yield a maximum strength-to-weight ratio, not maximum lean mass. As a rough blueprint, the prototypical climber's physique should resemble the powerful-looking upper body of a gymnast merged with the lean lower body of a distance runner. Of course, we each possess unique DNA, and we all will come to climb at a high level with somewhat different-looking body builds. Trust that by committing to an intelligent, long-term conditioning program, your physique will gradually morph into the best shape for optimal climbing performance.

The goal, then, of this chapter is to arm you with the basic knowledge needed to design and execute a most effective conditioning-for-climbing program. First, you will learn about the unique physical demands of climbing, including the specific roles that strength, power, endurance, and stamina play. Next, we'll take a look at the purposes of general and sport-specific conditioning, and examine the benefits and limitations of each method. The chapter concludes with a look at nine guiding principles of effective conditioning. The degree to which you abide by these principles will ultimately determine the quality of your results.

Conditioning for the Vertical Athlete

As a vertical athlete you are faced with many physical, technical, and mental challenges that come together into a complex matrix to be solved. In climbing near your limit, it's often difficult to determine which one of these performance-limiting constraints is holding you back. Consider that mental

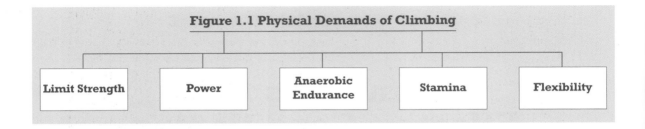

Figure 1.1 Physical Demands of Climbing

| Limit Strength | Power | Anaerobic Endurance | Stamina | Flexibility |

stress can trigger physical tension such as overgripping of the rock, just as poor technique or a missed foothold can cause the needless muscling of a move and a high burn rate of energy. The best climbers, of course, gradually refine their mental and technical abilities in order to move with utmost precision and fuel economy. So while elite climbers often appear to be tapping into some superhuman level of strength, what you can't readily see is the many years—often decades—they spent developing their exceptional climbing skills and mental acumen.

The key distinction here is that achieving excellence in climbing requires a commitment to work on all facets of the game—improving technique, refining mental skills, and increasing your level of physical conditioning. Many climbers make the mistake of concentrating only on physical training. It's the premise of *Conditioning for Climbers* that while physical training is important, you must also be dedicated to improving mentally and technically if you are ever to reach your full potential. Let's take a look at each of these topics.

Physical Demands of Climbing

The raw physical demands of climbing vary dramatically from route to route and with advancing grade of difficulty. While a beginner-level climb might be doable for an out-of-shape novice, an elite-level climb might require Herculean strength such as the capability to do a one-arm pull-up or climb 100 feet of overhanging wall without a rest. For the purposes of developing an effective training program, it's important to distinguish five types of physical demands (see figure 1.1).

■ LIMIT STRENGTH

Limit, or maximum, strength is fundamental to increasing almost all the physical capabilities required to improve your climbing. As you might expect, limit strength is the maximum force you can generate in a single all-out effort such as crimping on a minuscule handhold or pulling hard through a strenuous move. While such limit strength is only utilized on the most physical of climbing moves, it is very influential in determining your levels of power and anaerobic endurance. The importance of training limit strength cannot be overstated—it is fundamental to improving your climbing ability.

Ironically, exercises for building crucial limit strength are overlooked by many climbers. Popular body-weight exercises and the act of climbing do *not* build it, so there are big gains in limit strength awaiting most climbers. Chapters 6 and 7 will reveal several excellent limit-strength training exercises: hypergravity training, Heavy Finger Rolls, Uneven-Grip Pull-Ups, and more.

■ POWER

Power is the application of force with velocity—think of it as *explosive strength*—as in popping a deadpoint, making a fast pull and reach, or throwing a lunge. Power is a product of limit strength and the ability to rapidly activate a high percentage of fast-twitch muscle fibers. Therefore, power will increase with gains in limit strength and from explosive-strength-conditioning exercises that train synchronous muscle fiber recruitment. For example, speed exercises such as power pull-ups, one-arm lunging, and campus training are all valid for training power since they all demand rapid neuromuscular recruitment.

Matt Bosley using his power at Earth Treks, Timonium, Maryland.

PHOTO BY ERIC HÖRST

■ LOCAL, OR ANAEROBIC, ENDURANCE

When climbers talk about endurance, they are usually referring to anaerobic endurance local to the forearm and pull muscles, not the aerobic endurance needed for a long-distance run or full day of climbing. (Many climbers use the pseudo-term *power endurance* instead of *anaerobic endurance*.) Think of anaerobic endurance as the endurance of near-maximum strength needed to climb a continuously strenuous sequence without rests. For many climbers, failure on a route often seems to come down to a lack of local forearm endurance—although you must always consider whether lackluster technique and poor-quality thinking actually caused accelerated energy drain and premature muscular failure.

The hallmark of climbing or training in the anaerobic-endurance zone is the muscular pump and burn that develop. Your level of anaerobic fitness is a function of your limit strength, your muscles' ability to remove blood lactate, and your body's tolerance to the fatiguing effects of metabolic by-products such as lactic acid and ammonia. Effective training to improve anaerobic endurance must then concentrate on repeatedly exposing the muscles to high-intensity exercise and the elevated levels of metabolic by-products that result. Such interval training—with its alternating training burns separated by only brief rest periods—is the gold standard. Yes, it is painful and mentally grueling; however, it is a necessity to trigger the muscular adaptations that will increase local circulation and removal of lactic acid and other waste products. One of the key adaptations is an increase in capillary diameter and density within the muscles, and for this reason some climbers refer to this type of conditioning as *capillary training*.

■ STAMINA

Stamina is the ability to engage in physical activity for an extended period of time or even all day long. For the vertical athlete, stamina is a most important attribute if your preference is multipitch, big-wall, or alpine climbing. Conversely, stamina is subordinate to maximum strength and power when it comes to bouldering and sport climbing. These differences in physical demands underscore the importance of designing your conditioning program to be congruent with your climbing preference and goals.

There are two approaches to training stamina for climbing. The first and most effective strategy is to regularly log long days on the rock. Since this may not be possible for the weekend-only climber, engaging in traditional aerobic activities such as jogging, trail running, or mountain biking a few days per week is a beneficial substitute. Either way, a crucial stamina-training guideline is that exercise sessions must regularly push beyond what you are accustomed to. Do this two or three days per week, and you will soon be able to outlast almost any partner on the rocks.

■ FLEXIBILITY

While you will never need the extraordinary suppleness of a gymnast or dancer, proficiency at climbing does demand sufficient flexibility to execute fundamental techniques without undue stress or effort. Most important is lower-body flexibility as needed to stem, high-step, and hip turnout. Fortunately, climbing provides an excellent active stretching routine in and of itself. Climb three or four days per week and you will gain more functional flexibility. You can further increase flexibility with supplemental stretching exercises performed as part of your warm-up and cool-down ritual. As you will learn in chapter 3, all climbers can benefit from a few minutes of stretching and other warm-up activities. That being said, flexibility is rarely a limiting constraint on the rock, so it need not be the focus of intensive training. The majority of your conditioning program should concentrate on the physical demands of strength, power, endurance, and stamina.

Technical and Mental Demands

The physical demands of climbing are obvious, but the technical and mental demands are often more subtle—yet highly complex and even illusive for some climbers. While they are beyond the scope of this book, I would be remiss if I didn't stress the importance of all three aspects of what I call the Climbing Performance Pie (see figure 1.2). In working with hundreds of climbers over the years, I've

Figure 1.2 Climbing Performance Pie

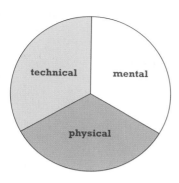

Perhaps more than any other sport, rock climbing requires equal mastery of the physical, mental, and technical domains.

observed that the majority were actually further ahead in their physical capabilities than they were in their technical and mental abilities (despite their belief to the contrary). This may or may not be your situation, and it's often quite difficult to discern your limiting constraints. This is where a self-assessment test (see chapter 2) or climbing coach comes in handy.

In summary, a training-for-climbing program will be most effective only if it addresses your greatest weakness, whether that be physical, mental, or technical. For most climbers, the optimal program will include some training and drills in all three areas. Consult my books *Learning to Climb Indoors* and *Training for Climbing* for comprehensive instruction on developing your mental and technical skills.

Types of Physical Conditioning

There are two types or categories of conditioning activities: general and sport-specific. Depending on your level of experience and conditioning, you may want to perform mostly general conditioning, mostly sport-specific conditioning, or a combination of the two.

General

The goal of general conditioning is to develop all-around fitness and the base level of strength needed to learn climbing moves and skills. Novice climbers would benefit from a period of general conditioning ranging from a few months to a year or two, depending on their level of fitness. A well-designed program would help improve cardiovascular fitness and stamina, optimize body composition through a reduction of percent body fat, and build strength in all the major muscle groups including the pull muscles that are so crucial to climbing. Such a general training program should be executed two or three days per week in addition to climbing once or twice a week. More information on general conditioning exercises and beginner-level programs is found in chapters 4 and 10, respectively.

Periodic general conditioning is also useful for advanced climbers. A few weeks of general strength training is beneficial after an extended layoff or at the beginning of a preseason conditioning program. Furthermore, it is advantageous for intermediate and advanced climbers to engage in frequent general conditioning of the antagonist push muscles, which over time tend to fall out of balance with the agonist pull muscles. Just ten to twenty minutes of antagonist muscle conditioning, twice per week, will improve muscle balance and lower risk of numerous upper-body injuries. See chapter 8 for a complete look at conditioning the antagonists.

Sport-Specific

As the name implies, this type of training targets the muscles, movements, and skills that are specific to our sport. Since upper-body conditioning is the most common physical constraint while climbing, a well-designed sport-specific program will train the muscles of the arms, forearms, back, and torso in ways that are very similar to climbing use. Exercises such as pull-ups or Lat Pull-Downs, One- or Two-Arm Lock-Offs, and Hanging Knee Lifts are all valid as sport-specific conditioning. And, since the fingers are the weakest link to the rock, it's crucial to engage in a variety of exercises to improve contact (maximum) grip strength and anaerobic endurance. A fingerboard, campus or HIT system, and small home bouldering wall all provide highly specific and, thus, supremely effective conditioning. Chapters 6 and 7

Thomas Blackford sending **Right El Danno (V6)**, *Coopers Rock, West Virginia.*

provide a comprehensive look at sport-specific conditioning of the finger and pull muscles.

The Basic Principles of Conditioning

Knowledge of the basic principles of physical conditioning empowers you to design a workout program that will be both maximally effective and time-efficient. While you may be familiar with a few of these principles from previous sports training, I urge you to consider how each principle can be uniquely applied to your conditioning-for-climbing program.

Warm-Up

The importance of a warm-up period is one of the few things that virtually all coaches and trainers agree upon. Five to fifteen minutes of light aerobic activity followed by a few minutes of mild stretching will increase the temperature and range of motion of the working muscles, as well as spread synovial fluid throughout the joints. The benefits of these adaptations include increased musculotendon function, improved joint articulation, and decreased risk of injury.

Individualization

This could also be called the snowflake principle, since it highlights that no two climbers—or their optimal conditioning programs—are the same. The best training program for you will target your specific weaknesses, address past or present injuries, provide sufficient time for recovery, and be structured to provide the greatest output for the available training input. Since there is no other climber quite like you, there is no other climber's conditioning program that you'd want to copy—doing so will provide less-than-optimal results and might even get you injured. *Conditioning for Climbers* will help you design the optimal program for you!

Specificity

The principle of specificity may be the most important of all for climbers to heed. It simply states that the more specific a training activity is to a given sport—muscle group, workload, velocity and pattern of movement, posture, and range of motion—

the more it will contribute to increasing performance in that sport. For an exercise to produce meaningful gains in functional strength and endurance for climbing, therefore, it must be markedly similar to climbing. Obviously, exercises that involve actual climbing motions (bouldering, fingerboard pull-ups, HIT workout, and such) are the most specific and will have the greatest transfer to climbing performance.

Effective training must also target the specific muscle fiber type and energy system most used in your preferred style of climbing. For instance, hard bouldering draws largely on fast-twitch muscle fibers and the ATP-CP energy pathway, so you want to favor brief, high-intensity exercises that target these constraints. Longer traditional or sport climbs, however, typically demand extended and alternating use of fast- and slow-twitch muscle fibers, with energy coming predominantly from glycogen stored in the muscles and liver. To specifically train these systems, you'd want to perform many high-repetition exercises or climb for mileage at the gym or crag.

Overload

This granddaddy of training principles states that in order to increase functional capacity for exercise, it is necessary to expose the neuromuscular and cardiovascular systems to a level of stress beyond that to which they are accustomed. You can achieve this overload by increasing the resistance and intensity, volume, and speed of training, or by decreasing the rest interval between successive sets. The best method of creating overload depends on the outcome you desire from your conditioning program. To excel in bouldering, for example, you'd want to create overload by increasing resistance and exercise intensity in order to build maximum strength and power. A roped climber would be more interested in developing local endurance and, thus, should create overload both by increasing exercise volume and by reducing rest intervals between exercise sets. Finally, a big-wall or alpine climber in need of greater stamina should train at a lower overall intensity and create overload by increasing total daily exercise volume.

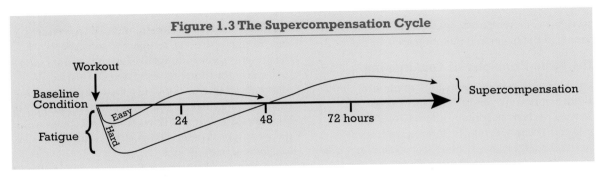

Figure 1.3 The Supercompensation Cycle

Recovery and supercompensation from a light workout may take as little as twenty-four hours, whereas it can take seventy-two hours or more to *fully recover and reach maximum supercompensation following a severe workout or day of climbing.*

Optimal Sets, Reps, and Rest Intervals Between Sets

While one set per exercise may be sufficient for a general conditioning program, it's widely accepted that performing two or three sets per exercise is needed to develop strength and power. Highly conditioned climbers engaging in an off-season strength-training program may benefit from as many as six sets of certain sport-specific exercises such as pull-ups, campus training, Heavy Finger Rolls, and such. However, two or three sets are ideal as supplemental in-season training performed in addition to actual climbing.

The optimal training load (resistance), reps performed, and rest interval between sets depend on the desired training outcome. Warm-up sets and general conditioning are best performed with a modest resistance that allows twenty to twenty-five repetitions. For the purposes of developing strength and power, however, select a high enough workload to produce muscular failure in just five to ten reps.

The length of rest between sets can similarly be managed to produce optimal training adaptations. A three- to five-minute recovery period is best when training for strength and power. A much shorter rest period—thirty seconds to perhaps two minutes—is optimal when training for local muscular (anaerobic) endurance, since it will limit the removal of metabolic by-products such as lactic acid. This training

protocol is indeed painful and mentally grueling. The payoff, however, is that over the course of several weeks your body will adapt for better removal of blood lactate as well as improving its capability to sustain function despite elevated blood lactate levels.

Order of Exercise

After performing a ten- to twenty-minute warm-up, it's best to commence with sport-specific exercises and conclude with more general supplemental training and aerobic activity. For example, any bouldering or wall climbing should have top priority—quality of movement is paramount when it comes to climbing activities, so you want to engage in such training when you are mentally and physically fresh. Upon completion of your climbing, move on to targeted supplemental exercises such as pull-ups, fingerboard exercises, campus training, HIT, and such. Follow this with general conditioning of the antagonist and core muscles, and finish up with aerobic training (or save it for a nonclimbing day).

Periodization

Periodization is the practice of varying workout focus, structure, intensity, and length every few days or weeks in order to maximize the training effect. If you do not use periodization, long-term consequences include a plateau in performance, boredom, and an increased risk of overtraining and injury. By training and climbing in the exact same ways and on the same schedule week after week, you are at risk of these undesirable outcomes. You can best employ periodization by planning your workouts ahead of time on a calendar or notebook, so that training focus and climbing preference change every few weeks. You can also incorporate a training mesocycle such as the 4-3-2-1 Cycle described in chapter 10.

Recovery

Muscular adaptations occur between, not during, workouts. Sufficient rest and healthy lifestyle habits (proper nutrition, adequate sleep, and the like) are fundamental to maximizing physiological adaptations to exercise. Depending on the intensity and volume of the training stimulus, the recovery process, known as supercompensation, typically takes anywhere from twenty-four to seventy-two hours (see figure 1.3). For example, it might only take one day to recover from a high volume of low-intensity activity like climbing several easy routes or an aerobic workout, whereas it often takes two or three days (sometimes more) to recover completely from a lengthy high-intensity workout such as climbing many routes near your limit or training maximum strength and power in the gym. Muscle soreness is a good estimate of recovery—if your muscles are sore, you have not recovered completely from your previous workout or day of climbing.

The importance of this principle cannot be overstated, since training too often—frequently climbing sore or tired—will eventually lead to a decline in performance and possibly injury. This is known as the overtraining syndrome, and it's unfortunately quite common among highly motivated climbers. Ironically, overtraining is the ultimate bad investment because it will eventually lead to a decrease in strength and performance—the opposite of the intended outcome!

Detraining

Upon cessation of strength training or frequent climbing, your level of maximum strength and local endurance will slowly erode after about ten to fourteen days of inactivity. A more significant decline in strength and endurance will occur in the weeks and months that follow, if training or climbing does not resume. While some downtime each year is a good thing (mentally and in the case of nagging injuries), frequent breaks in training of a week or more will make it difficult to acquire significant gains in conditioning.

Injuries are a common cause of unplanned breaks from training and a loss of physical conditioning. Fortunately, technical and mental skills wane very little, even during extended layoffs of a few months or more. Upon resumption of training, a return to peak physical conditioning may occur in as little as half the length of the layoff period. For example, two months of dedicated training should allow you to recapture the level of conditioning lost during a four-month layoff.

Self-Assessment and Goal Setting

Accurate self-assessment is an essential precursor to developing a conditioning program that really works.

The effectiveness of your conditioning-for-climbing program will be directly related to how well it targets your true weaknesses. For a beginning climber, weaknesses usually center on lack of climbing skill, fear of falling, and poor general fitness. More experienced climbers, however, tend to have specific areas of weakness, such as poor footwork, lack of confidence, or inadequate finger strength. Of course, there are many other skills and personal attributes that may be limiting your performance, and as a rule it gets more difficult to identify the limiting constraint as you advance in ability. Furthermore, your weaknesses change as you grow as a climber—so your limiting constraints are actually a moving target!

Regular self-assessment is a powerful tool to determine your true weaknesses so that you can accurately design a training program that works. On a micro scale, it's important to self-assess after every climb by asking yourself, *What could I have done better?* Similarly, you must occasionally take a wide-angle view of your climbing to identify persistent weaknesses and a possible stealth handicap that you may not be aware of. A climbing coach is a tremendous resource for obtaining an objective analysis of your mental, technical, and physical weaknesses. A self-assessment test is similarly useful for a quick evaluation of your overall game. A well-designed assessment will break down the spectrum of climbing performance into specific elements, thus highlighting your strong and weak areas.

This chapter provides you with an eight-part self-assessment that targets the critical areas of climbing experience, technical skills, mental skills, general conditioning, sport-specific conditioning, injury risk, nutrition, and lifestyle. Each part consists of five questions worth a total of 25 points. Compare your scores in each part to identify the two or three areas most holding you back—these would be the lowest scoring parts of the assessment. Similarly, survey your answers question by question to identify specific weaknesses that should become the bull's-eye of your conditioning program.

In taking this assessment, it's best to read each question once and then immediately select an answer. Don't read anything into the questions, and resist the common tendency to cheat up on your scores. Circle the answer that most accurately describes your current abilities and modus operandi.

Honed veteran climber Rick Fleming sending the classic **Bullet the New Sky (5.12b),** *New River Gorge, West Virginia.*

PHOTO BY ERIC McCALLISTER

Evaluate Your Climbing Experience

1. How long have you been climbing?
   1—less than six months
   2—six to twelve months
   3—one to four years
   4—five to ten years
   5—more than ten years

2. On average, how many days per month do you climb (both indoors and outdoors)?
   1—one day or less
   2—two or three days
   3—four to eight days
   4—nine to twelve days
   5—more than twelve days

3. How many different climbing areas and gyms have you visited in the last year?
   1—just one
   2—two to four
   3—five to nine
   4—ten to fifteen
   5—more than fifteen

4. How many of the following styles of climbing have you been active in over the last year: bouldering, gym climbing, sport climbing, follow trad climbs, leading trad climbs, big walls?
   1—one or two
   2—three
   3—four
   4—five
   5—six

5. How many of the following types of climbing have you engaged in over the last three months: slab climbing, face climbing, crack climbing, overhanging face climbing, pocket climbing, roofs?
   1—one or two
   2—three
   3—four
   4—five
   5—six

Analysis

Add up your scores for each question and record your total score here: _____. Use the scale below to assess your level of climbing experience.

23–25: You are well on your way to mastery!

20–22: Your experience is above average.

15–19: Your experience is average.

10–14: Your experience is limited or narrow in scope, but huge gains await you given a commitment to climb more often and explore new types of climbing.

5–9: As a novice climber you possess tremendous potential to improve. A regular schedule of climbing and a willingness to stretch your boundaries will yield rapid gains in ability.

Set Goals

Review the questions on which you scored 3 or less, then set a specific goal for improvement in each area. Write down what actions you plan to take and a time frame for attaining this goal. For example, if you scored three or fewer points on question 3, you could set a goal to visit ten new climbing areas in the next year.

Set goals for broadening and deepening your experience:

Evaluate Your Technical Skills

1. My footwork and overall technique deteriorate during the hardest part of a climb.
   1—almost always
   2—often,
   3—about half the time
   4—occasionally
   5—seldom or never

2. Cracks, slabs, and roofs feel hard for the grade compared with a similarly graded face climb.
   1—almost always
   2—often
   3—about half the time
   4—occasionally
   5—seldom or never

3. I have difficulty finding midroute rest positions and shakeouts.
   1—almost always
   2—often
   3—about half the time
   4—occasionally
   5—seldom or never

4. On the typical climb, I feel like much of my body weight is hanging on my arms.
   1—almost always
   2—often
   3—about half the time
   4—occasionally
   5—seldom or never

5. On overhanging routes and roofs, I have difficulty finding the optimal body position or keeping my feet from cutting loose.
   1—almost always
   2—often
   3—about half the time
   4—occasionally
   5—seldom or never

Analysis

Add up your scores for each question and record your total score here: _____. Use the scale below to assess your level of technical skills.

23–25: You possess excellent technical skills!

20–22: Your technical skills are above average.

15–19: Your technical skills are near average; however, the next level is attainable given a focused effort to improve in weak areas.

10–14: You possess some fundamental flaws in climbing technique. Make improving your technique a top priority. Consider employing a coach to provide technical instruction and tips for improvement.

5–9: You are at the beginning of the learning curve. With a consistent schedule of climbing, you will see rapid gains in ability.

Set Goals

Review questions on which you scored 3 or less, then set a specific goal for improvement in each area. Write down what actions you plan to take along with a time frame for attaining this goal. For example, if you scored 3 or fewer points on question 1, make it a goal to constantly focus on your footwork and to resist the tendency to muscle through difficult moves.

Set goals for improving your technique:

Evaluate Your Mental Skills

1. I visualize myself successfully climbing the route before I leave the ground.
   1—seldom or never
   2—occasionally
   3—about half the time
   4—often
   5—almost always

2. I get anxious, tight, and hesitant as I climb into crux sequences.
   1—almost always
   2—often,
   3—about half the time
   4—occasionally
   5—seldom or never

3. I miss hidden holds or blow a known sequence.
   1—almost always
   2—often
   3—about half the time
   4—occasionally
   5—seldom or never

4. I make excuses for why I might fail on a route before I even begin to climb.
   1—almost always
   2—often
   3—about half the time
   4—occasionally
   5—seldom or never

5. When lead climbing a safe route, I push myself to the complete limit and, if I fall, I fall trying.
   1—seldom or never
   2—occasionally
   3—about half the time
   4—often
   5—almost always

Analysis

Add up your scores for each question and record your total score here: _____. Use the scale below to assess your level of mental skills.

23–25: You possess excellent mental skills!

20–22: Your mental skills are above average.

15–19: Your mental skills are near average; however, significant gains are attainable given a commitment to mental training.

10–14: Your limited mental skills are an Achilles' heel that's sabotaging your climbing performance. Desire and discipline to improve in this area will yield huge breakthroughs in climbing ability.

5–9: Your weak mental skills will improve rapidly given a regular schedule of climbing and a willingness to stretch your boundaries and challenge your fears.

Set Goals

Review questions on which you scored 3 or less, then set a specific goal for improvement in each area. Write down what actions you plan to take along with a time frame for attaining this goal. For example, if you scored 3 or fewer points on question 1, commit to the goal of inspecting and visualizing every route before leaving the ground.

Set your mental-training goals:

Evaluate Your Level of General Conditioning

1. How many pounds (body fat or excessively bulky muscles) do you estimate you are from your ideal climbing weight?
   1—more than twenty
   2—ten to twenty
   3—five to ten
   4—just a few
   5—zero

2. How far could you jog (modest-paced steady running) without stopping?
   1—less than 0.5 mile
   2—0.5–1 mile
   3—1–2 miles
   4—3–5 miles
   5—more than 5 miles

3. How many pull-ups can you do in a single set?
   1—women: one or none, men: fewer than five
   2—women: two to four, men: five to nine
   3—women: five to nine, men: ten to nineteen
   4—women: ten to twenty, men: twenty to thirty
   5—women: more than twenty, men: more than thirty

4. How many push-ups can you do in a single set?
   1—women: two or fewer, men: fewer than five
   2—women: three to six, men: five to fifteen
   3—women: seven to fifteen, men: sixteen to twenty-five
   4—women: sixteen to twenty-five, men: twenty-six to forty
   5—women: more than twenty-five, men: more than forty

5. How many Abdominal Crunches can you do in a single set using the technique shown on page 61?
   1—fewer than ten
   2—ten to twenty
   3—twenty-one to forty-nine
   4—fifty to seventy-five
   5—more than seventy-five

Analysis

Add up your scores for each question and record your total score here: _____. Use the scale below to assess your level of general conditioning.

23–25: You possess excellent general conditioning!

20–22: Your general conditioning is above average.

15–19: Your general conditioning is near average. Improvement in this area will facilitate better movement and improved stamina and reduce injury risk.

10–14: Your general conditioning is below average and is undoubtedly limiting your climbing ability. See chapter 4.

5–9: You possess poor general conditioning. It's paramount that you improve in this area before engaging in a regular schedule of climbing. See chapter 4.

Set Goals

Review questions on which you scored 3 or less, then set a specific goal for improvement in each area. Write down what actions you plan to take along with a time frame for attaining this goal. For example, if you scored 3 or fewer points on question 1, set a weight-loss goal and commit to a regular schedule of aerobic activity.

Set your general conditioning goals:

Evaluate Your Sport-Specific Conditioning

1. On overhanging routes with large holds, I pump out quickly and need to hang on the rope.
   1—almost always
   2—often
   3—about half the time
   4—occasionally
   5—seldom or never

2. I have difficulty hanging on small, necessary-to-use holds.
   1—almost always
   2—often
   3—about half the time
   4—occasionally
   5—seldom or never

3. I find it difficult to hold a lock-off with one arm when I let go to advance the other hand.
   1—almost always
   2—often
   3—about half the time
   4—occasionally
   5—seldom or never

4. Given a marginal midclimb rest, I can shake out and recover enough to complete the route.
   1—seldom or never
   2—occasionally
   3—about half the time
   4—often
   5—almost always

5. My maximum bouldering ability is:
   1—V0 or V1
   2—V2 to V3
   3—V4 to V5
   4—V6 to V7,
   5—V8 or above

Analysis

Add up your scores for each question and record your total score here: _____. Use the scale below to assess your level of sport-specific conditioning.

23–25: You possess excellent sport-specific conditioning!

20–22: Your sport-specific conditioning is above average.

15–19: Your sport-specific conditioning is near average; however, a program of targeted training will quickly elevate you to the next level.

10–14: Your sport-specific conditioning is a major constraint in climbing performance. If you are an intermediate or advanced climber, vow to increase your commitment to this type of training. If you are a novice, however, continue general conditioning for another year or so before beginning sport-specific conditioning.

5–9: You possess a poor level of conditioning. Engage in a general training program for at least one year before initiating a sport-specific conditioning program.

Set Goals

Review questions on which you scored 3 or less, then set a specific goal for improvement in ach area. Write down what actions you plan to take along with a time frame for attaining this goal. For example, if you scored 3 or fewer points on question 5, make it a goal to go bouldering more frequently to benefit from the targeted training it provides.

Set your sport-specific conditioning goals:

Evaluate Your Injury Risk

1. I perform a warm-up activity and some stretching before climbing or training.
   1—seldom or never
   2—occasionally
   3—about half the time
   4—often
   5—always

2. I climb hard on three or more consecutive days.
   1—every week
   2—often
   3—a couple times per month
   4—once per month
   5—seldom or never

3. When climbing, I experience elbow, shoulder, or finger pain.
   1—almost always
   2—often
   3—occasionally
   4—infrequently
   5—never

4. I engage in regular training of the antagonist push muscles.
   1—never
   2—infrequently
   3—a few times a month
   4—once or twice a week
   5—twice a week, religiously

5. I stop climbing or end a workout prematurely if I experience unusual joint or tendon pain.
   1—never
   2—infrequently
   3—about half the time
   4—often
   5—always

Analysis

Add up your scores for each question and record your total score here: _____. Use the scale below to assess your potential risk of injury.

23–25: Congratulations: Your injury awareness and risk mitigation practices make you less susceptible than average to a climbing injury.

20–22: Kudos to you, too, for doing what it takes to reduce injury risk.

15–19: You are at near-average risk of a climbing injury. Just a small commitment to warm-up activities, planned recovery, and antagonist muscle training will significantly lower your risk.

10–14: You are at above-average risk for overuse or acute climbing injuries. Strive to be more proactive with injury prevention.

5–9: You are at high risk for an injury while training or climbing. Review each question to determine what actions you can take to lower your risk.

Set Goals

Review questions on which you scored 3 or less, then set a specific goal for improvement in each area. Write down what actions you plan to take along with a time frame for attaining this goal. For example, if you scored 3 or fewer points on question 4, commit to training your antagonist muscles twice per week.

Set goals for decreasing your risk of injury:

Evaluate Your Nutritional Habits

1. How often do you eat breakfast?
   1—never
   2—weekends only
   3—three days a week
   4—five days a week
   5—every day

2. How often do you eat fast food or fried food?
   1—four or more days per week
   2—two to three days per week
   3—once a week
   4—once or twice per month
   5—less than once per month

3. On average, how soon after a workout or the end of your climbing day do you consume some carbohydrate and protein?
   1—more than three hours
   2—two to three hours
   3—one to two hours
   4—thirty minutes to one hour
   5—within thirty minutes

4. How many servings of fruits and vegetables do you consume per day?
   1—zero or one
   2—two
   3—three
   4—four
   5—five or more

5. How often do you plan out your meals ahead of time for the purpose of eating for performance and optimal recovery?
   1—seldom or never
   2—once per week
   3—two or three days per week
   4—four to six days per week
   5—every day

Analysis

Add up your scores for each question and record your total score here: _____. Use the scale below to assess the quality of your nutritional habits.

23–25: You possess excellent nutritional habits!

20–22: Your nutritional habits are above average.

15–19: Your nutrition is near average, but improving your habits will boost your energy, stamina, and recovery times.

10–14: Your diet is below average. Strive to eliminate this constraint on your climbing performance and recovery ability by improving dietary surveillance throughout the week.

5–9: Your poor nutritional habits are both a health risk and a constraint on climbing performance. Make it a priority to make permanent changes in this area—it will improve your quality of life as well as your climbing.

Set Goals

Review questions on which you scored 3 or less, then set a specific goal for improvement in each area. Write down what actions you plan to take along with a time frame for attaining this goal. For example, if you scored 3 or fewer points on question 3, make it a high priority to consume some protein and carbohydrate within the first hour after training or climbing.

Set your nutritional goals:

Evaluate Your Lifestyle and Discipline

1. How many days per week do you engage in a physical activity such as climbing, training, or another sport?
   1—one
   2—two
   3—three
   4—four
   5—five

2. On average, how many hours sleep do you get each night?
   1—less than five
   2—five to six
   3—six to seven
   4—seven to eight
   5—more than eight

3. How often do you pig out eating and drinking with little restraint?
   1—three or more days per week
   2—twice per week
   3—once per week
   4—once or twice per month
   5—seldom or never

4. Do you smoke?
   1—more than a pack a day
   2—less than a pack a day
   3—only socially
   4—I quit
   5—I've never smoked

5. When you set goals or begin a workout program, how often do you follow through to successful completion?
   1—seldom
   2—occasionally
   3—about half the time
   4—often
   5—almost always

Analysis

Add up your scores for each question and record your total score here: _____. Use the scale below to assess your lifestyle and level of self-discipline.

23–25: You are a highly disciplined individual and well on your way to mastery!

20–22: Your discipline is above average and a real asset to your climbing.

15–19: Your discipline is near average. Try to identify one or two areas in which you can strive for improvement.

10–14: Your below-average discipline is a constraint on your climbing. If you are serious about climbing better, resolve to adjust your lifestyle and subordinate less important activities.

5–9: Your lifestyle and lack of discipline are definitely holding you back. Determine your priorities, and make the lifestyle changes needed to elevate your score to 15 or above.

Set Goals

Review questions on which you scored 3 or less, then set a specific goal for improvement in each area. Write down what actions you plan to take along with a time frame for attaining this goal. For example, if you scored 3 or fewer points on question 2, determine what low-value activities (such as socializing, watching TV, or surfing the Net) you might reduce or eliminate to allow for more sleep each night.

Set your lifestyle and discipline goals:

_____

_____

_____

_____

_____

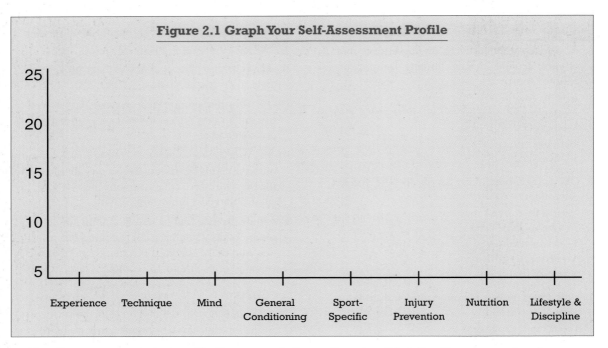

Figure 2.1 Graph Your Self-Assessment Profile

25

20

15

10

5

Experience | Technique | Mind | General Conditioning | Sport-Specific | Injury Prevention | Nutrition | Lifestyle & Discipline

Creating your assessment profile. Upon completing and scoring this full self-assessment package, it's beneficial to plot the results to obtain a graphical profile. Using figure 2.1, draw bar graphs according to your score in each part of the package. Take note of your three shortest bars. These low-scoring areas represent the greatest constraints on your climbing performance.

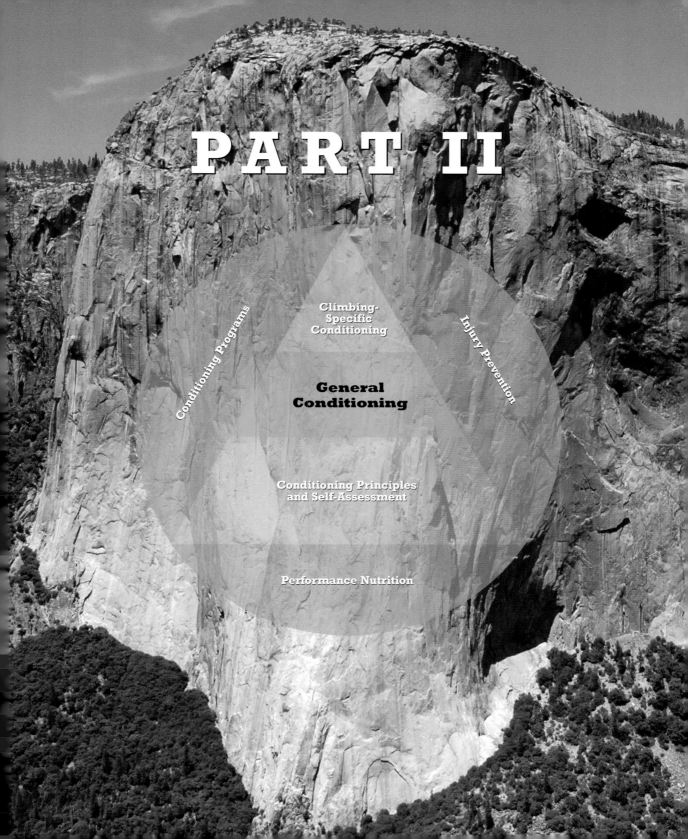

PART II

**General
Conditioning**

Climbing-
Specific
Conditioning

Conditioning Programs

Injury Prevention

Conditioning Principles
and Self-Assessment

Performance Nutrition

Warm-Up Activities and Flexibility Conditioning

Consider that movement is the very essence of the vertical dance we call climbing. From this perspective, there should be no debate that warm, flexible muscles and joints will facilitate smooth, efficient movements.

While strength and endurance are common constraints on difficult climbs, it's rarely apparent that lack of flexibility is limiting factor. But just because it's not apparent doesn't mean it's not a very real factor affecting your performance. Let me state in no uncertain terms that possessing a modest level of flexibility and engaging in a preclimb warm-up *will* enhance performance, albeit in a number of subtle ways that you may not recognize.

Consider that movement is the very essence of the vertical dance we call climbing. From this perspective, there should be no debate that warm, flexible muscles and joints will facilitate smooth, efficient movements. Furthermore, warm muscles function better both in terms of force production and through a lessening of inherent resistance in the antagonist muscles that oppose the prime movers.

*Climber on **The Great Escape** (5.10d), Shagg Crag, Maine.*

PHOTO BY ERIC McCALLISTER

Finally, there's the payoff of reduced injury risk and increased rate of recovery. Given all these benefits, why would any climber not engage in a routine of warm-up activities and stretching before every workout or climbing session? It should be as obvious a thing to do before climbing as chalking up and tying into a rope!

Gleaning the benefits of warm-up and flexibility activities does not require a large time investment or much energy. As little as ten to twenty minutes per day will provide all the benefits listed above. This chapter will arm you with more than twenty-five highly effective warm-up movements and stretches for your fingers, arms, neck, torso, hips, and legs. You can maximize your results by performing every stretch in this chapter—in the order they are presented—and by following the stretching guidelines provided in the Tips for Safe and Effective Stretching box on page 40.

Warm-Up Activities

There are several warm-up activities that you should engage in before moving on to targeted stretching of the climbing muscles. The best strategy is to begin with a general warm-up activity to increase heart rate and body temperature. Next is a series of arm and torso movements to warm individual muscles and spread synovial fluid through the joints. Following these activities, you'll be ready to engage in a period of safe and productive stretching of the arms, legs, and torso.

General Warm-Up

The first and most important step of the warm-up process is to engage in a brief period of light aerobic activity. While five minutes of steady, light exercise is sufficient for increasing blood flow and core temperature, many climbers discover that they perform better after ten to fifteen minutes of aerobic activity. Many climbing gyms are equipped with a stationary bike, treadmill, or elliptical trainer, all of which are ideal for the purpose of a general warm-up. You could also go for a short run, jump rope for five minutes, or do one hundred jumping jacks—all good alternatives if you are training in a home gym. Upon breaking a light sweat, you can move on to specific warm-up movements described below.

Finger Curls

This warm-up movement is the most important for climbers, because it warms the many joints of the hands and helps increase circulation to the forearm muscles. Always perform Finger Curls before engaging in any forearm stretching.

1. Stand with your arms relaxed by your sides.

2. Close your hands to make a relaxed fist, and then quickly open your hand and fan out the fingers as if trying to flick water off your fingertips.

3. Continue for thirty to forty repetitions. Use a pace that allows about two repetitions per second.

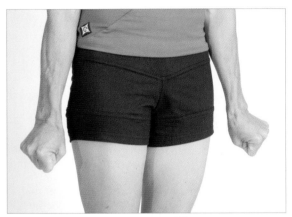

Make a relaxed fist.

Quickly open and fan fingers.

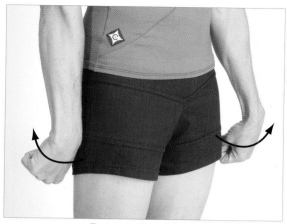

Rotate relaxed fists.

Wrist Circles

This motion warms the wrist joint and increases circulation to the forearm muscles.

1. Stand with your arms by your sides.

2. Make a relaxed fist with both hands, and circle your hands through a comfortable range of motion for ten repetitions.

3. Switch directions and perform another ten Wrist Circles.

Arm Circles

This movement warms the shoulder joints and increases circulation to the muscles of the shoulders and arms.

1. Start with your arms out to the sides and parallel to the floor.

2. Begin moving your arms in small circles. Gradually increase the size of the circle until you feel slight tension in your shoulders—go no larger with the circles than this.

3. Use a moderate pace, so that each circle takes about one second to complete.

4. Complete twenty circles, then switch direction and perform another twenty circles.

Safety notes: Do not wildly whip your arms or swing them in any way that hurts your shoulders. Strive for a smooth, gentle motion throughout.

Extend arms to sides, then rotate arms in circles.

Arm Scissors

This is an excellent movement for warming up the many large muscles of the chest, shoulders, and upper back.

1. Start with your arms out to the sides and parallel to the floor.

2. Begin moving your arms forward until they pass across each other in a scissorlike motion. Stop the motion at the point the arms cross each other at about a 90-degree angle.

3. Immediately reverse direction and move your arms back out to the sides until they pass just beyond the plane of your body. Cease the motion at the first sign of tension in your shoulders.

4. Continue this scissorlike motion for a total of twenty to thirty repetitions. Use a modest pace that takes one to two seconds per rep.

Safety notes: Do not swing your arms wildly, and don't force the range of motion beyond comfortable limits.

Extend arms parallel to floor.

Crisscross arms in a scissorlike motion.

Shoulder Shrugs

This movement is wonderful for releasing tension from the often tight muscles of the neck, shoulders, and upper back. When done properly, you will feel a stretch at the top and bottom of the movement.

1. Stand with arms relaxed by your sides and your head straight.

2. Raise your shoulders up toward your ears, rolling them slightly backward at the top of the movement.

3. Lower your shoulders back to the starting position and then press them toward the floor.

4. Continue this up-and-down shrug motion at a slow, controlled pace, taking about two seconds per repetition.

5. Perform a total of twenty to thirty shrugs.

Raise shoulders upward and roll them backward.

Relax arms.

Neck Circles

This movement will further warm up and relax the many small muscles of your neck.

1. Stand with your arms relaxed by your sides and your head straight.

2. Start by dropping your chin to your chest, then begin a slow, gentle clockwise movement that takes about two seconds per complete circle.

3. Do ten circles, then change direction to perform ten head circles in the counterclockwise direction

Safety notes: Do not race through this movement, and don't force an unnatural range of motion. It's important to only move your head in a circular motion and not in a front-and-back, nodding motion.

Drop chin.
Gently rotate head.

Hula Hoop

This is a great movement for loosening your hips and back joints.

1. Stand with your feet shoulder width apart. Let your arms hang loosely by your sides—or you can place them on your hips.

2. Flex slightly in your knees and begin rotating your hips in a circular motion, as if you're playing with a hula hoop. Maintain a nearly still head and shoulders throughout.

3. Continue for fifteen seconds, then switch directions and rotate for another fifteen seconds.

Rotate hips in a circle.

Switch directions.

Back Roll

This final movement improves spine flexibility and warms the abdominal and lower-back muscles.

1. Sit with your knees bent and feet flat on the floor.

2. Extend your arms forward and grab your knees. Relax through your arms, but try to maintain good sitting posture.

3. Pull your knees toward your chest and roll backward until your shoulders touch the floor. Immediately rock back up to the starting position, striving for smooth, steady movement throughout the range of motion.

4. Continue for fifteen to twenty repetitions.

Safety note: Err on the side of rolling too slowly through the range of motion. You never want to do fast, ballistic warm-up movements.

Wrap arms around knees.

Roll backward, then up to starting position.

Upper-Body Stretches

Climbing places high demands—and sometimes potentially injurious levels of stress—on the many muscles of your arms, shoulders, chest, and back. To begin climbing without first thoroughly warming and stretching these upper-body muscles is, thus, foolish and tempts injury. Use the following eight stretches to best prepare these muscles and joints for peak performance and injury avoidance.

Finger Flexors

This is the most basic stretch for climbers, since it works the forearm muscles that enable finger flexion and your grip on the rock. Perform the stretch in the two positions described below.

1. Stand with arms relaxed by your sides.

2. Bring your arms together in front of your waist. Straighten the arm to be stretched and lay the fingertips into the palm of the opposite hand. Position the hand of the stretch arm so that it's oriented palm-down with the thumb pointing inward.

3. Pull back on the fingers of your straight arm until the stretch begins in your forearm muscles. Hold this stretch for about twenty seconds.

4. Release the stretch and turn your hand 180 degrees so that your stretch arm is now positioned with the palm facing upward and the thumb pointing outward.

5. Again using the opposite hand, pull the fingers back until a stretch begins in the forearm muscles. Hold for twenty seconds.

6. Repeat this stretch, in both positions, with your other arm.

Stretch with thumb inward.

Stretch with thumb outward.

Finger Extensors

This important stretch is unfortunately overlooked by many climbers. It stretches and warms up the extensor muscles of the back of the forearm; when done religiously, it will help prevent lateral tendinosis (often called tennis elbow).

1. Stand with your arms relaxed by your sides.

2. Bring your arms together in front of your waist. Straighten the arm to be stretched, make a tight fist, and place it in the palm of your other hand.

3. With your fist hand in the thumb-up position, gently pull the fist inward to create a mild stretch along the back of your forearm.

4. Hold this stretch for ten seconds, and then slowly rotate your forearm to work the stretch for an additional ten seconds with the fist turned to the thumb-down position.

5. Repeat this stretch with your other hand.

Stretch in thumb-up position.

Stretch in thumb-down position.

Stretch bent fingers one at a time.

Stretch between each pair of fingers.

Finger Isolation

This isolation stretch, along with massage of the fingers and hands, is very effective for warming up your precious digits. Work through this sequence one finger at a time.

1. Either sitting or standing, bend one arm at the elbow to position your hand palm-up at chest level.

2. Curl your fingers about three-quarters of the way, but do not close your hand or make a fist.

3. Extend your hand into a hand-back position.

4. Place the index finger of your other hand across the last digit of the finger to be stretched, then position your thumb under the finger near your hand knuckle.

5. Gradually apply pressure with your index finger to further close the bent finger and to push it back in the direction opposite to which it flexes. Stop when you feel mild tension in the joints.

6. Hold this stretch for ten seconds. Release the finger for a few seconds and repeat the stretch for another ten to twenty seconds.

7. Repeat this process with all eight fingers.

Safety notes: Stop immediately if you experience any pain. Also, do not use this stretch on a recently injured finger or if you have significant arthritis of the hands.

Finger Split

Here's another good stretch before your fingers start levering off pockets or twisting in finger cracks.

1. Either sitting or standing, bend one arm at the elbow to position your hand thumb-up at chest level. Keep your hand in a straight, neutral position, and fan the fingers wide open.

2. Bunch up the fingers of the other hand and place them between two of your fanned-out fingers. Gradually expand the bunched-up fingers to force the two fanned-out fingers farther apart. Stop when you feel mild tension.

3. Hold this stretch for ten seconds. Release for a few seconds, then repeat for another ten to twenty seconds.

4. Repeat this stretch with each pair of fingers.

Safety notes: Stop immediately if you experience any pain. Also, do not use this stretch on any finger with a recent ligament or joint injury.

Rhomboids and Trapezius

This is a great stretch for the shoulder and upper-back muscles that are so heavily used in climbing vertical and overhanging walls.

1. From a standing position, bring one arm across your chest until the hand rests on your opposite shoulder. Maintain the bent elbow at chest level so that your arm is parallel to the floor.

2. With your other hand, grasp behind the bent elbow from below.

3. Pull on the bent elbow across your chest until you feel tension in the shoulder and upper back.

4. Hold the stretch for ten seconds. Release for a few seconds before repeating for twenty seconds more.

5. You can stretch the shoulder muscles more completely by slowly working the bent elbow up and down a few inches from the horizontal position.

6. Repeat this stretch with your other arm.

Pull elbow across chest until you feel tension.

Triceps

This stretch targets the triceps while also producing a mild stretch of the shoulders and lat muscles of the back.

1. Stand erect with your arms overhead and bent at the elbows.

2. Grab one elbow and gently pull it toward the back of your head until you feel a stretch in the back of the upper arm.

3. Hold the stretch for ten seconds. Release for a few seconds, then perform a secondary stretch for about twenty seconds.

4. You can extend this stretch down through your shoulder and back by leaning sideways slightly in the direction that you're pulling your elbow.

5. Repeat this stretch with your other arm.

Pull elbow toward back of head until you feel tension.

Biceps

This is an excellent stretch that targets the biceps as well as the chest and shoulders.

1. Sit on the floor with your feet flat and knees bent about halfway.

2. Position your arms just behind your hips with your elbows straight, palms flat, and fingers pointing back.

3. Slowly walk your hands away from your hips until you feel mild tension in your biceps.

4. Hold this position for twenty seconds.

5. Walk your fingers back a few inches farther to increase the tension a bit more. You may also feel some mild stretching in your shoulders and chest. Hold this position for twenty to thirty seconds before releasing the stretch.

Walk hands away from hips.

Deltoids and Latissimus

This is a great finishing stretch of the many muscles in the chest, shoulders, and upper back.

1. Begin down on all fours and walk your hands forward to a position about a foot in front of your shoulders.

2. Maintaining straight arms, lower your chest toward the floor until you feel slight tension develop in the muscles of your shoulders and chest. You can enhance the stretch by shifting your hips slightly backward.

3. Hold this stretch for ten seconds, then raise upward slightly to release the tension for a few seconds.

4. Perform a secondary stretch lasting twenty to thirty seconds.

Safety note: Apply just enough downward pressure to provide mild tension throughout the muscles of your arms and upper torso. Immediately ease up if you feel any pain in your elbows or shoulders.

Lower chest until you feel tension in shoulders.

Tips for Safe and Effective Stretching

- Always engage in a few minutes of warm-up activities before beginning your stretching. Jogging, jumping rope, cycling, jumping jacks, or any other activity that increases your heart rate will work.

- Stretch in a slow, gradually progressive manner. Never bounce or do any motion that is forceful or painful. Stretching should produce some discomfort, but never pain.

- Perform a primary stretch of ten to twenty seconds. Release the stretch for a few seconds before performing a secondary stretch for twenty to sixty seconds. Favor the longer stretch intervals for the large muscles of the lower body.

- An alternative stretch method, known as proprioceptive neuromuscular facilitation (PNF), replaces the period of relaxation between the primary and secondary stretches with a period of muscular contraction. For most of the stretches described below, you will need a partner to create an immovable resistance against which you can contract for six seconds. After this isometric contraction, relax completely and allow the stretch to lengthen the muscle. This is an especially useful technique for those trying to overcome uncommon lack of flexibility.

- Concentrate on the area you're stretching. Focus on relaxing the muscle and visualize tension escaping like air from a balloon.

- Maintain slow, deep breathing throughout the stretch. Inhale through your nose and exhale through your mouth.

- Maintain a neutral back position—neither rounded nor hyperextended—to maximize the stretch and avoid injury. Avoid old-school stretches like toe touching and hurdlers' stretch—they will forcefully round your lower back and tempt injury.

- Stretch all the muscles groups to keep the agonists and antagonists in balance. Resist the tendency to stretch only the (agonist) pull muscles—climbing uses *all* muscle groups!

- To obtain best results, engage in some stretching five or six days per week, and not just on climbing days. However, it's essential that you always engage in a period of warm-up activity prior to stretching. *Never* stretch a cold muscle!

Lower-Body Stretches

While leg strength is rarely a limiting factor in rock climbing, lack of lower-body flexibility can be, at times, a limitation. For example, dihedrals and overhanging routes often require the ability to stem widely between holds, while overhangs and steep face climbs often demand high steps and heel hooks.

A modest level of flexibility is an asset on such climbs; in fact, limber, nimble legs and hips will help facilitate smooth, efficient movement on all routes regardless of type and grade. Why not, then, spend five or ten minutes stretching the large and commonly taut muscles of the lower body? Following are eight useful stretches to put to work beginning today!

Buttocks and Lower Back

This stretch will improve hip flexion and help facilitate high-stepping.

1. Lie flat on your back with both legs straight.

2. Grasp one leg behind the thigh, and pull it toward your chest.

3. Hold the stretch for ten seconds, then release it for a few seconds.

4. Pull the thigh toward your chest again for a secondary stretch of about twenty seconds.

5. Repeat with the other leg.

Pull bent leg toward chest and hold.

Hamstrings

The muscles along the back of the thigh are chronically tight in many climbers, thus restricting stem and high-step movements. Daily use of this stretch will yield significant improvement.

1. Lie flat on your back with one leg straight and the other bent slightly.

2. Lift the straight leg upward, grab it behind the thigh or calf, and pull gently forward until you feel the stretch down the back of your leg.

3. Hold this stretch for ten seconds, then release it slightly for a few seconds.

4. Pull the leg once again for another twenty- to thirty-second stretch. Be sure to maintain a straight leg all the while.

5. Repeat with your other leg.

6. Alternatively, loop a fitness band over your foot and regulate the stretch by pulling on the band.

Pull straight leg forward and hold.

Piriformis

The piriformis muscle lies deep beneath the gluteal muscles, and it assists in lifting and rotating the thigh laterally. In climbing, you use this muscle to position your foot on a hold that's up and out to the side. If you have trouble reaching out your foot to engage distant edges, a tight piriformis is likely part of the problem. The piriformis stretch may also provide some relief for individuals experiencing mild sciatica.

1. Kneel on the floor with your hands positioned under your shoulders.

2. Shift your upper-body weight onto your arms, so that you can reposition your legs as follows.

3. Move one leg in front of you, keeping the knee sharply bent so that the heel is positioned near your groin.

4. Slide the other leg backward until it's straightened out behind you. Your kneecap should be facing down to the floor while the sole of your foot faces up toward the ceiling.

5. Use your arms to align your torso over the center of your bent leg. Lower your hips toward the bent leg to increase the stretch. Hold this position for ten seconds, then raise your hips slightly to release the stretch for a few seconds.

6. Lower your hips once more for a secondary stretch of thirty to sixty seconds. Most people feel a strangely pleasant stretching deep within the gluteal muscles.

7. Repeat with your other leg.

Safety notes: Perform this stretch with caution and ease up at the first sign of any pain in your knees, hips, or lower back. This stretch may be inappropriate for individuals with a history of knee injuries.

Lower hips and hold.

Adductor

This wall stretch is one of the very best lower-body stretches for climbers. Lying on the floor eliminates strain on the lower back and allows you to relax and let gravity do the work. Wearing socks can reduce friction between your heels and the wall, helping maximize your range of motion.

1. Lie on the floor with your buttocks about 6 inches from a wall and your legs extending straight up it, with a 90-degree bend at your hips.

2. Slowly separate your legs by sliding your heels out to the sides. Concentrate on relaxing throughout your body and allow gravity to extend the split until you feel mild tension in your legs and groin.

3. Hold this position for ten to twenty seconds.

4. Try to split your legs farther apart; if needed, grab your thighs to apply some downward pressure to extend the stretch.

5. Hold this position for thirty to sixty seconds.

Separate legs, relax, and let gravity extend split.

Groin

This stretch, known as the Froggie or Butterfly, is excellent for improving hip turnout. Flexibility gains from this stretch will allow you to move your center of gravity in closer to the wall—more over your feet—on near-vertical climbs.

1. Sit upright with your legs flexed and your knees out to the sides so that you can bring the soles of your feet together.

2. Grasp your ankles and rest your elbows on the insides of your thighs.

3. Press down with your elbows to apply light pressure on your thighs until you feel mild tension in your groin and inner thigh. Hold this stretch for ten seconds, then release it for a few seconds.

4. Apply pressure for a secondary stretch of twenty to thirty seconds.

5. Next, lie down flat on your back while keeping your feet together.

6. Relax and allow gravity to pull your knees toward the floor for another thirty seconds to one minute.

Gently press elbows down on thighs.

Lie flat and allow gravity to pull knees downward.

Quadriceps, Groin, and Hip Flexors

Another great stretch that works many muscles through your upper legs, groin, and hips.

1. Kneel on the floor with one leg forward and bent at near 90 degrees, while the other leg is extended behind you.

2. Lean slightly forward and place your hands on your knee or on the floor near your lead foot.

3. Maintaining a nearly straight rear leg and flat spine, slowly lower your hips a few inches toward the floor until you feel tension in the groin and quadriceps. Hold this position for ten seconds, then raise your hips slightly to release the stretch for a few seconds.

4. Lower your hips to perform a secondary stretch for twenty to thirty seconds.

5. Switch leg positions and repeat the stretch.

Shift hips forward until you feel tension.

Quadriceps and Hip Flexors

This is a great quadriceps stretch and one of the kindest to the knee joints. Note, however, that proper technique requires use of the hand opposite the leg you're stretching.

1. Kneel on one leg; place the other leg in front of you with a 90-degree knee bend and your foot flat on the floor.

2. Steady yourself by leaning slightly forward and touching the ground on either side of your forward leg or by resting your hand on your knee.

3. Reach back with the hand opposite the kneeling leg and firmly grasp that foot with your hand atop the laces part of your shoe.

4. Gently pull forward on your foot while you also slide your hips forward. Apply just enough pressure to feel moderate tension develop in the quadriceps of your kneeling leg.

5. Hold this for ten seconds, then release for a few seconds.

6. Stretch again for another twenty to thirty seconds.

7. Repeat with your other leg. Remember to switch hand positions.

Pull foot forward with opposite hand until you feel tension.

Calf

The gastrocnemius and soleus muscles of the calf are the unsung heroes of climbing performance. These muscles provide support for the never-ending edging, smearing, jamming, and front pointing that carries most of our weight up the rock. Stretching these workhorse muscles before and after every climbing session should be considered mandatory—it will improve performance and recovery, respectively.

1. Starting down on all fours, lift your knees off the floor and press your hips toward the ceiling to attain an inverted-V body position.

2. Relax one leg and bring it slightly forward while the other leg remains straight.

3. Press the heel of the straight leg down so your entire shoe sole is in contact with the floor. You will begin to feel light tension in your calf muscles.

4. Increase the stretch by shifting your hips forward. Hold this for twenty seconds, then lift your rear heel off the floor for a few seconds of relaxation.

5. Again press your heel back to the floor to produce a secondary stretch for thirty to sixty seconds. Maintain heel contact with the floor throughout.

6. Repeat with the other leg.

Press back heel to floor and shift hips backward, then forward.

Lower Back and Buttocks

This final lower-body stretch is very sport-specific and will leave you ready to go climbing. The high leg position and erect posture produce a deep stretch in your buttocks and lower back that will improve your high-stepping ability.

1. Stand along the front of a table or chair with your feet shoulder width apart and turned out to the sides.

2. Lift one leg—as in high-stepping—and place the sole of that foot atop the table or chair with the foot pointing out to the side, as if it were edging on a foothold.

3. Slowly rock over your high foot until you feel a stretch in your buttocks, groin, and lower back. Hold this for ten seconds, then shift your weight back to center to relax the stretch for a few seconds.

4. Slowly shift your weight back toward the high leg to stretch for another twenty seconds.

5. Repeat with the other leg.

Safety notes: Do not use a table or chair higher than your hip level. A table of normal height—between 26 and 32 inches high—works best for most individuals. Cease stretching if you feel any unusual pain in your groin, lower back, hips, or knees.

Stand with high foot turned outward, shift weight over it, and hold.

Torso/Core Stretches

Whether you know it or not, the muscles of your core are at work with every climbing move you make. This group of muscles surrounds your torso from the shoulders, chest, and upper back down along your abdomen and spine to near your pelvis, hips, and lower back. This chain of muscles maintains proper posture, produces body tension, and transfers power and torque from upper to lower body, and vice versa. The importance of properly warming up and stretching these muscles should be obvious to any serious climber.

Bend to side and hold.

Obliques

This is an excellent first stretch for the core muscles of the torso and, in particular, the external obliques.

1. Stand with your feet shoulder width apart.

2. Bend your arms directly overhead. With each hand, grip your the opposite elbow.

3. Lean slowly sideways until you feel mild tension along the side of your trunk. Bend at the waist, while remaining still below the waist. Don't lean forward or backward, only sideways.

4. Hold this stretch for ten seconds, then return to the starting position for a few seconds.

5. Perform a secondary stretch for another twenty seconds.

6. Repeat this stretch toward the other side.

Abdominals

Climbing works the abdominals as much as any other muscle group in the body. Consider this a mandatory stretch both before and after climbing.

1. Lie flat on the floor with your arms bent and your palms flat next to your shoulders.

2. Slowly press your shoulders away from the floor until you feel mild tension in your abdominals. Keep your legs and pelvis in contact with the floor for the duration of this stretch—it helps to contract your buttocks in order to maintain this position and reduce stress on your lower back.

3. Hold the stretch for ten seconds, then return to the starting position for a few seconds.

4. Press upward for a secondary stretch of twenty to thirty seconds. Relax and allow the curve of your spine to extend up through your upper back and neck. Look forward, but not up toward the ceiling.

Safety notes: Do not be overly aggressive with this stretch—proceed with caution, especially if you have a history of back problems. Stop immediately if you experience any pain in your lower back.

Press shoulders up and away from floor; contract buttocks.

Trunk Rotation

Climbing contorts your body along three axes: front-to-back, side-to-side, and rotationally along a vertical axis. This stretch and the final one, below, will help prepare your body for the torso-twisting, hip-turning, drop-kneeing movements that are ubiquitous during indoor and sport climbs.

1. Sit erect on the floor with one leg straight and the other bent and crossing over your opposite knee.

2. Slowly turn your body toward the side of the bent leg until you feel mild tension in your lower back, your hips, and the side of your torso. Maintain a level head position and fix your eyes on the wall to the side of your bent leg.

3. Hold the stretch for ten to twenty seconds, then return to the starting position for a few seconds.

4. Perform a secondary stretch for twenty to thirty seconds. If needed, you can increase the stretch by levering your elbow against the thigh of the bent leg.

5. Repeat the stretch in the other direction. Be sure to switch leg positions.

Safety note: Use caution in performing this or any rotational stretch. Stop immediately if you experience pain in your hips or spine.

Gently rotate torso toward bent-leg side.

Lower Back and Hips

This is a great finishing stretch for the torso and lower body, because it works several muscle groups of the core, hips, and legs.

1. Lie flat on your back with your arms out to the sides.

2. Lift and bend one leg until it is flexed at a 90-degree angle at both the hip and knee.

3. Raise the arm opposite your bent leg and grip near that knee.

4. Pull the knee across your body and toward the floor until you feel tension in your lower back, hips, or thigh. Keep your head and both shoulders flat on the floor.

5. Hold the stretch for ten to twenty seconds, and then return to the starting position for a few seconds.

6. Perform a secondary stretch, this time pulling the bent knee all the way to the floor (or until mild tension develops). Hold this position for twenty to thirty seconds.

7. Repeat the stretch with your opposite leg, pulling it to the other side.

Safety note: Proceed carefully, and stop immediately if you experience any pain in your hips or spine.

Gently pull knee toward floor. Keep shoulders flat on floor.

Basic Conditioning and Weight Loss

Since there is no other climber quite like you, there is no other climber's conditioning program that you'd want to copy. You possess unique strengths and weaknesses, experience, genetics, and goals, so your optimal program will be unlike that of any other climber.

Developing movement skills and enjoying a day of climbing requires a certain base level of physical fitness. For example, if you cannot climb several beginner-level routes without incurring significant fatigue, then poor general fitness is a primary constraint that will limit your potential to improve as a climber.

One benchmark of general fitness for climbing is your strength-to-weight ratio, or how well you can perform specific exercises at your current body weight. Measurements of this ratio include how many pull-ups and push-ups you can perform and, to a lesser extent, how fast and far you can run. Obviously, excessive body fat is a liability, whereas well-conditioned yet not excessively bulky muscles are an asset. Good cardiovascular conditioning is

The author on-sighting **The Green Ripper** *(5.12b), Mt. Lemmon, Arizona.*

PHOTO BY ERIC McCALLISTER

also advantageous, because it enhances recovery ability and overall resistance to fatigue while you train and climb. Improving in all these areas is the focus of this chapter.

To begin, you will learn several effective body-weight exercises to perform a few days per week at home or at the gym after climbing. These basic training exercises are not particularly specific to climbing; they are, however, ideal for novice or out-of-shape climbers looking to upgrade their physical capabilities. As an alternative to the body-weight exercises, we'll also examine the use of circuit training with exercise machines or free weights. The chapter concludes with a review of the important subject of body composition and weight loss. In terms of increasing strength-to-weight ratio, training to reduce excessive body fat or muscle mass is as valid as—and perhaps more easily achieved than—increasing muscular strength. It's important that all climbers consider both sides of the strength-over-weight fraction, and then train to improve in both areas.

Body-Weight Exercises

In chapter 2 you assessed your level of general conditioning using several body-weight exercises as metrics. These same exercises are also your tools for improving general physical fitness. Perform the following exercises three days per week, either at home as part of a training day or at the climbing gym at the end of your session. Retake the general conditioning self-assessment (in chapter 2) every three months and modify your training program as follows:

- Upon reaching a score of 15 points, begin to introduce some of the sport-specific training exercises contained in part 3 of this book.

- With a score of 20 or greater, you can cease general training and focus exclusively on sport-specific training activities.

Pull-Up

The pull-up is the most universal exercise used by climbers, and it should be a staple of your general fitness-training program. Perform your pull-ups on a bar, the bucket hold of a fingerboard, or a set of free-hanging Pump Rocks. Use the next two exercises (Aided Pull-Ups and the Lock-Off and Lower) if you are unable to do at least eight pull-ups.

1. Mount the bar or board with your hands in a palms-away position (the way you usually grip the rock) and about shoulder width apart.

2. Pull up at a relatively fast rate in order to reach the top position in one second or less. Pause at the top for just a moment, and then lower yourself to a two-second count. Subvocalize, *one thousand one, one thousand two.*

3. Upon reaching the bottom position, immediately begin your next pull-up.

4. Continue in this fashion until you can no longer perform a complete pull-up.

5. Do three to five sets with a rest interval of at least three minutes between sets.

6. As your pull-up strength improves, begin to vary the distance between your hands to better simulate the wide range of hand positions you'll encounter in climbing.

Pull up for one second; lower for two seconds.

Aided Pull-Ups

A conundrum for some beginning climbers is how to train pull-up strength if they can't do a pull-up! Fortunately, there are two highly effective exercises that will help you over this hurdle in a matter of weeks. The first strategy is simply to have a spotter hold you around your waist and lift a portion of your body weight so that you can do eight to ten less-than-body-weight pull-ups. Use this exercise three days per week, and soon you'll be doing pull-ups on your own!

1. Mount the bar or hangboard with your hands in a palms-away position, about shoulder width apart.

2. With the spotter standing behind you and holding you lightly around your waist, begin doing pull-ups. The spotter should provide help only on the upward phase of the pull-up.

3. Pause for a moment at the top, then lower to a slow two-second count. The spotter should let go during the down phase so that you are lowering full body weight.

4. Continue doing pull-ups in this manner until you reach eight to ten total repetitions.

5. Rest for five minutes, then perform two more sets.

Lock-Off and Lower

If you do not have a spotter available to help you (as needed for Aided Pull-Ups), you can similarly train your pull muscles by lowering through the down phase of the pull-up and just skipping the upward phase. Here's how.

1. Place a chair below the pull-up bar or hangboard and step up into the top position with your hands pulled in near your armpits.

2. Remove your feet from the chair and maintain a lock-off at this top position for two seconds before slowly lowering yourself to a five-second count. Subvocalize, *one thousand one, one thousand two,* and so on, trying to sustain a slow descent that takes five seconds.

Spotter helps lift a portion of body weight on upward phase only.

3. Upon reaching the bottom, straight-armed-hang position, step back up on the chair to reach the top again.

4. Hold another lock-off at the top position for two seconds before beginning another slow-motion descent.

5. Continue in this fashion for a total of five to ten repetitions. Stop the exercise if you can no longer lower yourself at a slow, controlled rate. Never allow yourself to drop uncontrolled into the straight-armed position.

6. Perform a total of three sets with a five-minute rest between sets.

Push-Ups

This popular gym-class exercise is actually a great exercise for climbers to use in strengthening their shoulder and chest muscles. Performing two sets of standard push-ups, two or three days per week, will help prevent some of the shoulder injuries that climbers commonly experience.

1. Lie facedown on the floor with your arms bent and your hands flat on the floor near your armpits.

2. Stiffen your torso muscles just enough to create body tension so that you can maintain a straight body position as you begin your push-ups.

3. Push up to the straight-armed (top) position, and immediately return to the bottom position.

4. Without pause, continue the up-and-down motion at a brisk pace that takes just one to two seconds per repetition. No resting between reps!

5. Continue until you can no longer push up to the top position. If you are able to do more than twenty-five reps, increase the difficulty by moving your hands a few inches closer together for the next set and for future workouts. The most difficult way to do push-ups is with your hands overlapped directly below your sternum.

6. Perform one or two more sets with a three- to five-minute rest between sets.

Beginner's note: If you cannot perform at least ten push-ups in the manner described above, you should then do the push-ups with your knees remaining on the floor to lower the resistance. In a few weeks you'll gain enough strength to do at least the first set with your knees off the ground.

Push yourself up . . .

. . . and down without pause.

Bench Dip

Dips are an excellent exercise for strengthening the triceps, deltoids, pectorals, and the many smaller stabilizer muscles of the upper body. Of course, the dip motion is similar to that of pressing out a mantle move on the rock, so you have double the reason to perform this exercise two or three days per week. Most health clubs have apparatuses similar to the parallel bars for performing dips, but at home you'll need to be a little more creative. For general conditioning I advocate using the Bench Dip, but I suggest that you progress to dipping on a set of free-floating Pump Rocks or gymnastics rings (see page 140 in chapter 8) as you advance in ability.

If you haven't done dips before, you will discover that they are surprisingly difficult. Initially, strive to do two sets of six to twelve repetitions, with the long-term goal of fifteen to twenty reps. To further increase the difficulty of this exercise, you can elevate your feet by resting your heels on the edge of a chair positioned a few feet in front of you.

1. Begin by sitting on the edge of a bench or sturdy chair, your feet flat on the floor. Securely grip the edge of the bench with the palms of your hands pressing on the top of the bench.

2. Press down with your hands and lift your rear end off the bench. Walk your feet a foot or two forward so that your hips shift to a position a few inches in front of the bench.

3. Slowly lower your hips toward the floor by bending your arms. Stop when your arms are bent at a 90-degree angle, then immediately push back up to the top position.

4. Continue this up-and-down motion at a steady pace that takes just one to two seconds per repetition.

5. Return to the seated position on the bench when you feel that you can no longer control your motion or complete another dip. Rest for three to five minutes.

6. Perform one or two more sets with an additional three- to five-minute rest between sets.

Safety note: Never lower yourself below a 90-degree arm position.

Begin with straight arms.

Lower until upper arm is parallel to floor, then push back up.

Side Squat

This body-weight exercise is highly effective for training many of the lower-body muscles you use in climbing. Perform fifteen to thirty repetitions and I'm sure you'll begin to feel a burn in your quadriceps. The Side Squat also works the gluts, adductors, abductors, hamstrings, and the muscles of your calves. Fortunately, body-weight squats will strengthen your leg muscles without adding bulk—important for climbers.

1. Stand with your feet a bit more than shoulder width apart. The farther apart they are, the harder this exercise will be.

2. Bend your arms slightly and hold them just in front of your hips. You'll need to subtly shift your arms to maintain balance while performing this exercise.

3. Slowly bend your left leg and begin shifting your center of gravity to the left as you lower yourself over your left foot.

4. Now press back up with your left leg to return to the starting position. Maintain a straight right leg throughout this down-and-up motion.

5. Immediately begin another repetition with the same leg. Continue for fifteen to thirty repetitions, or stop when you can no longer control your downward motion.

6. After a brief rest, perform a set with your right leg doing the squatting motion.

Place feet at shoulder width-plus.

Lower yourself over one foot, then push back up.

Abdominal Crunch

Chapter 5 provides a detailed look at strengthening the important core muscles of the torso. As an ice-breaker, let's examine the most basic exercise, the Abdominal Crunch—a safer, more effective version of the traditional sit-up we all learned in grade school.

1. Lie on the floor with your legs bent at about 90 degrees and your feet flat on the floor. Cross your arms over your chest or place your hands behind your head (harder), but do not interlace your fingers behind your neck.

2. Now lift your shoulder blades off the floor and exhale as you "crunch" upward. The range of motion is small—the goal is to lift your upper back off the floor, but *not* to ascend the whole way as you would in old-school sit-ups.

3. Continue this up-and-down motion at a brisk pace that takes just over one second per repetition—but don't go so fast that you are bouncing off the floor!

4. Perform as many crunches as possible. Your long-term goal should be fifty to seventy-five reps.

5. Rest for five minutes, then execute a second set. As your conditioning improves, you can perform a third set as well.

Safety note: When performing crunches with hands behind your head, it's important never to pull on your neck or head.

Lie flat, legs bent, with hands behind head.

Exhale while crunching halfway up. Do not pull on your neck or head.

Circuit Training

If you have access to a health club or well-equipped climbing gym, you can engage in a circuit-training program as an alternative to the body-weight exercises described above. The goal of your circuit training is *not* to lift maximally heavy weights or to build big muscles—don't get drawn down that path!—but instead to simply acquire the modest level of fitness needed to climb regularly, learn skills, and reduce injury risk. You can gain all these upsides from a modest time investment of about forty-five minutes, three days per week. Per chapter 3, engage in ten to fifteen minutes of warm-up activities beforehand, and then conclude your workout with about twenty minutes of aerobic activity. This ninety-minute workout represents an excellent general conditioning program.

The accompanying sidebar lists the primary circuit training exercises to perform—ask an instructor for help should you be unsure how to do a specific exercise or uncertain how to set up or adjust a specific machine. Initial workouts will require a little experimentation to find the right training weight for you on each machine. The ideal weight will allow you to perform fifteen to twenty repetitions before reaching muscular failure—I do not advise using the standard health-club, bodybuilding protocol of doing eight to ten repetitions. Upon finding the correct exercise weight on each machine, stick with it until your newfound strength enables you to crank out more than twenty reps. Upon reaching this benchmark, simply increase the weight five to ten pounds for future workouts. Consider keeping a written record of your weights and reps so you can track your improvements.

After three months of circuit training, it's time to retake the general conditioning self-assessment in chapter 2 and modify your program accordingly:

• If you reach a score of 15 points, then you can begin to introduce some of the sport-specific training exercises contained in part 3 of this book.

• Score 20 or more points and you can cease circuit training in favor of exclusively climbing-specific training activities.

Circuit Training Exercises

Perform two sets of each exercise listed below. Select a weight that produces muscular failure in fifteen to twenty repetitions. Execute each exercise slowly and without stopping in the middle of a set—continuous muscular tension throughout the entire set is critical for maximizing the training effect. Count *one thousand one* on the upward phase of each repetition and *one thousand one, one thousand two* on the way down. Take a one- to two-minute rest between sets.

1. Bench Press
2. Shoulder Press
3. Pec Fly
4. Lat Pull-Down
5. Upright Rows
6. Triceps Extension
7. Biceps Curl
8. Leg Press
9. Leg Extension
10. Leg Curl
11. Rotary Torso
12. Abdominal

Weight-Loss Strategies

If you've ever hiked with a heavy pack or carried someone on your back, you've experienced the negative effects of increased weight on physical performance. Conversely, a reduction in percent body fat or unnecessary muscle mass will have a profoundly positive effect on performance. As mentioned earlier, strength-to-weight ratio is the best single metric of your conditioning for climbing. While much of this book focuses on increasing strength, we must also examine the other side of the coin: reducing weight.

First, I must state that I am an advocate of slow, reasonable weight loss. Crash dieting in pursuit of a gaunt, ultraskinny physique not only is dangerous but will ultimately have a negative effect on your climbing as well. A reasonable weight-loss target is to achieve a percent body fat of between 6 and 12 for men, or 8 and 16 for women. If you're not sure how you measure up, consider having your body fat tested at a local health club or university training center. Otherwise, use the simple pinch-an-inch method on your waistline. If the skin fold you pinch is an inch or greater in thickness, then you are definitely not in the optimal ranges listed above and will benefit noticeably from a reduction in percent body fat. A skin fold of 0.5 to 1 inch indicates body fat slightly above the optimal range and, thus, the need to lose just a few pounds. If you possess a skin fold of 0.5-inch or less, you are in the optimal range and not in need of weight loss.

Although myriad books have been written on this subject, the fact is that the prescription for weight loss is simple. Two principles represent the alpha and the omega of weight loss:

• To lose weight, your daily calorie intake must be less than your total daily calorie expenditure. Regardless of where the calories come from—fat, carbohydrate, protein, alcohol—your daily "net" must be negative. The best strategy is to both reduce caloric intake *and* increase daily expenditure.

• Diets don't work. Whether you diet for a week or a month, you will gain back all the weight when you go off the diet. Individuals who succeed in permanent weight reduction aren't really on a diet but have instead made fundamental changes in the way they eat that are *permanent*.

Let's examine the two sides of the weight-loss coin: reducing caloric consumption and increasing expenditure of calories.

Nutritional Surveillance

Nutritional surveillance is about increasing awareness of what, where, when, and why you eat. The goal is to reduce empty calories consumed via junk foods, high-fat fast foods, and such, while maintaining steady consumption of protein and carbohydrate, as well as water- and fiber-rich fruits and vegetables. The ideal macronutrient caloric breakdown for an athlete is 65 percent carbohydrate, 15

percent protein, and 20 percent fat. Consequently, you can dismiss the high-fat fad diets such as the Zone or Atkins—these are absolutely the wrong eating strategies for an athlete, whose primary source of energy is carbohydrate!

As an example, an active 160-pound male desirous of some weight loss might restrict his total dietary intake to around 2,550 calories per day (consuming up to 50 percent more calories on extremely active days). According to the 65/15/20 macronutrient profile for climbers, this would break down to about 415 grams of carbohydrate, 96 grams of protein, and just 56 grams of fat. Similarly, an active 130-pound female wanting to drop a few pounds might limit her total daily consumption to about 1,700 calories (up to 50 percent more on extremely active days), striving for a macronutrient breakdown of around 275 grams of carbohydrate, 64 grams of protein, and just 38 grams of fat. Upon achieving your desired climbing weight, gradually increase caloric intake to determine the level at which you can maintain a stable body weight. Of course, every individual has a unique basal metabolic rate and therefore different caloric needs—the values above are just sample estimates.

In striving to improve nutritional surveillance, it's important to begin reading food labels and never eat anything without knowing the precise fat and calorie content. Remember that a gram of fat contains 9 calories, while a gram of protein and a gram of carbohydrate each contain just 4 calories. Therefore, it's your ability and desire to control fat consumption that will most readily make or break your nutritional goals. The simplest step for dropping some unwanted pounds is to avoid high-fat foods and in particular foods containing saturated fats and trans fats—start reading food labels and you may be surprised to see how many foods contain these killer fats. However, you do not need to stop eating all dairy and animal products. Simply select the low-fat varieties such as skim milk (an excellent source of protein), grilled chicken or fish, and extra-lean cuts of steak. See chapter 12 for more tips on performance nutrition.

Determining Your Caloric Needs and Weight-Loss Prescription

Your caloric needs are a function of your metabolic rate, body weight, and the amount and intensity of exercise you perform.

- If you have a slow metabolism, multiply your body weight (in pounds) by 12. The total is your daily "maintenance" caloric need if no exercise is performed.

- If you have a midrange metabolism, multiply your body weight by 15.

- If you have a high metabolism, then multiply your body weight by 18.

Add 150 calories for each hour of low-intensity exercise; for example, an hour of walking at work or school burns about 150 extra calories per day. High-intensity exercise, such as climbing near your limit or running hard, can burn 600 calories or more per hour of sustained exercise. Therefore, forty-five minutes of aggregate climbing time or trail running would burn approximately 450 calories above your basic metabolic rate.

As an example, a 160-pound person with a midrange metabolism who walks one hour per day and climbs a total of forty-five minutes in aggregate would burn: (160 x 15) + 150 + 450 = 3,000 calories on that day. Now calculate your daily caloric needs using this method—or use the Web calculator at www.trainingforclimbing.com/new/calorie_calculator.shtml.

Determining a Reasonable Calorie Deficit for Producing Weight Loss

For the 160-pound climber, a modest caloric restriction of 15 percent below daily maintenance would yield a target value of 2,550 calories. Eating 2,550 calories per day while expending an average of 3,000 calories yields a 450-calorie deficit. Given the discipline to maintain this exercise and nutrition schedule for eight consecutive days, the result would be a 3,600-calorie deficit and a legitimate weight loss of just over one pound. It's important to note that a scale might register a weight loss of more than one pound, but any additional "loss" is water weight, which fluctuates up and down from day to day.

Determine the ideal amounts of each macronutrient given your daily calorie target amount.

In the above example, a 160-pound climber wanting to restrict intake to 2,550 calories per day would want to consume roughly the following amount of each macronutrient:

• Carbohydrate:

2,550 x 0.65 = 1,658 calories
1,658 calories ÷ 4 calories per gram =
~ 415 grams of carbohydrate

• Protein:

2,550 x 0.15 = 382 calories
382 calories ÷ 4 calories per gram =
~ 96 grams of protein

• Fat:

2,550 x 0.20 = 510 calories
510 calories ÷ 9 calories per gram =
~ 56 grams of fat

Aerobic Conditioning

The goal is to perform twenty to forty minutes of an aerobic exercise that elevates your heart rate to between 65 and 85 percent of maximum. Calculate your maximum heart rate by subtracting your age from 220. For example, a thirty-five-year-old has a maximum heart rate of 185 beats per minute; calculating 65 to 85 percent of this maximum rate prescribes an optimal training zone of 120 to 157 beats per minute.

You get maximum benefits from your aerobic exercise by maintaining a heart rate within this zone for the full duration of exercise. No matter the method, increase the intensity or speed of training if your heart rate is below this zone. Conversely, you should slow down (but not stop) immediately should your heart rate exceed the high end of the training zone. The easiest way to monitor heart rate is to take a fifteen-second count of heartbeats from your wrist, then multiply this number by four to get the one-minute total. Do this every three to five minutes during your aerobic exercise.

When it comes to aerobic exercise, running is by far the most effective method of incinerating fat and shrinking unwanted muscle. Don't worry about losing your climbing muscles—they will be preserved as long as you continue to climb regularly and consume at least 1 gram of protein per kilogram of body weight per day. Other popular aerobic activities such as mountain biking and the StairMaster will yield mixed results: They do eat up body fat, but they also tend to maintain (or build) undesirable leg muscle. Swimming, brisk hiking, and the use of an elliptical trainer (or similar) are good alternatives if you can't run.

Frequency and length of aerobic training should be proportional to the magnitude of your weight-loss goal. For example, a daily twenty- to forty-minute run is an important part of your training-for-climbing program if you are significantly overweight. As you near ideal weight, however, just two or three twenty-minute runs per week would be sufficient.

Guidelines for General Fitness Conditioning

- Concentrate on improving body composition and all-around fitness. Moderate aerobic training (such as running) and basic conditioning exercises will effectively build base fitness.

- Favor body-weight exercises such as pull-ups, push-ups, dips, and Abdominal Crunches over machines or free weights.

- Perform some modest training of the push muscles to maintain muscular balance, since the pulling muscles will steadily grow stronger as a result of climbing.

- Engage in regular stretching to improve flexibility and reduce injury risk.

- Climb two to four days per week to develop climbing strength. For the time being, resist the urge to engage in the high-intensity, sport-specific exercises commonly used by more advanced climbers.

Running is one of the most effective weight-loss strategies.

PHOTO BY RANDY LEVENSALER, WWW.LEVENSALER.COM

Core-Muscle Conditioning

In rock climbing the core muscles play a key role in enabling your arms and legs to maximize leverage and transfer torque from hand to foot and vice versa. In fact, every full-body climbing movement calls the core muscles into action.

Talk of core conditioning is in vogue these days, and the six-pack-abs look is indeed highly coveted by climbers and nonclimbers alike. But there's more to the core than meets the eye. Think of your core as the area between your shoulders and hips, a region that serves as the foundation for all physical movement. Given this understanding, we realize that while stunning abs may be the hallmark of the core, they are but one of many different muscle groups that contribute to a strong, stable core.

In rock climbing the core muscles play a key role in enabling your arms and legs to maximize leverage and transfer torque from hand to foot and vice versa. Furthermore, the core muscles are what provide body tension when you're trying to make a long reach or twisting body movement. In fact, every full-body climbing movement calls the core muscles into action. Consequently, a lack of core conditioning makes executing climbing moves harder—a performance overcharge—especially when venturing onto steep terrain. So if you fre-

quently struggle on vertical to overhanging routes, it's a safe conclusion that your difficulties are due to a combination of poor technique and insufficient upper-body and core conditioning.

So what's the best method of training these muscles? Sit-ups or abdominal crunches are the obvious choices; however, these exercises target only a small portion of your core muscles. Other popular options are yoga and Pilates classes, which bring all the muscles of the torso into play. Despite the rigors of these classes—which are excellent for developing body awareness, flexibility, and general conditioning—they may fail to develop a high level of climbing-specific core strength. So while participating in yoga or Pilates classes is a worthwhile endeavor, there remains a need to engage in supplemental core training that activates the core muscles in more strenuous and climbing-specific ways.

Frequently climbing on steep terrain is an excellent way to strengthen core muscles, though some climbers may be in a catch-22 situation of not having enough strength to adequately train on steep terrain. If this sounds familiar or if you are new to climbing, then a commitment to regular core training will be time well invested. More advanced climbers can similarly benefit from supplemental core conditioning—in particular, the total-core exercises described late in this chapter may prove challenging and advantageous.

This chapter provides four categories of core exercises to select from in planning your workouts. While there's no need to perform all sixteen exercises in a given workout, you should pick two or three from each group. Make a commitment to engage in core conditioning three to five days per week, and you will build a solid foundation from which you can climb your best.

*L.A. perusing **The Good Book** (5.10a), New River Gorge, West Virginia.*

PHOTO BY ERIC J. HÖRST

Abdominals and Obliques

The following five exercises each trains the abdominals and obliques in a somewhat different way.

Select three of these exercises for each workout, including at least one that works the obliques. Vary the exercises used from session to session.

Feet-Up Crunches

The crunch is the single most popular exercise for strengthening the abdominal muscles, and it should rightly be a staple of your core-training program. This feet-up version of the crunch excels in isolating the upper abdominals and reduces strain on your lower back.

1. Lie on the floor with your legs bent at about 90 degrees and your feet hovering in the air about knee height above the floor.

2. Cross your arms over your chest or place your hands behind your head (harder), but do not interlace your fingers behind your neck.

3. Now lift your shoulder blades off the floor and exhale as you "crunch" upward. The range of

motion is small—the goal is to lift your upper back off the floor, but not to ascend all the way to your knees as you would in old-school sit-ups.

4. Continue up and down at a brisk pace that takes just over one second per repetition—but don't go so fast that you are bouncing off the floor!

5. Perform as many crunches as possible. Your long-term goal should be fifty to seventy-five repetitions. As your conditioning improves, you can perform a second set after a three-minute rest.

Safety note: When performing crunches with hands behind your head, it's important to never pull on your neck or head.

Let feet hover at about knee height.

Exhale while crunching halfway up.

Seated Knee-Ups

This basic exercise works the abdominal muscles in addition to the hip flexors and numerous stabilizing muscles of the core.

1. Sit on an armless chair, stool, or weight-lifting bench. Rest your feet flat on the floor and grip the bench with your hands positioned just behind your hips.

2. Hold your knees and feet together, lean your shoulders and head back slightly, and lift your feet off the floor.

3. Pull your knees toward your chest until your heels reach the same level as the bench, and then lower them to within a few inches of the floor.

4. Continue this knee-up motion at a slow, steady pace, taking about two seconds per repetition.

5. Terminate the exercise when you can no longer lift your heels to bench level or if you are unable to maintain a stable position on the bench.

6. Rest for three minutes before performing a second set or moving on to the next abdominal exercise.

Safety note: Skip this exercise if you experience lower-back pain or have a history of lumbar spine injury.

Pull knees toward chest.

Leaning back, lift feet off floor.

Hanging Knee Lifts

This strenuous exercise targets the lower abdominal muscles in a very climbing-specific way—much like lifting your legs on an overhanging route.

1. Mount a pull-up bar, the bucket holds of a fingerboard, or a set of Pump Rocks with your palms facing away.

2. Briskly lift your knees up to your chest level, allowing your legs to bend naturally with the motion.

3. Pause for a moment, and then lower your legs slowly until they return to a slightly bent position.

4. Immediately begin the next upward repetition, and continue this knee-lift motion at a steady pace until you can no longer perform the full range of motion. Your long-range goal is to do twenty-five to thirty repetitions.

5. Rest for three minutes before performing a second set or moving on to the next abdominal exercise.

Safety note: To prevent sustained, full loading of the shoulder joints, it's important to maintain some tension in your arm and shoulder muscles throughout this exercise. Think about slightly contracting the muscles of your upper arms, shoulders, and chest as you execute the knee lifts.

Hang with arms straight.

Lift knees to chest level.

Oblique Crunches

Although only slightly different from the crunches described above, this exercise targets the obliques and will produce a unique muscular burn along the side of your abdominals.

1. Lie on the floor with your legs bent and torso twisted so that your knees are lying off to one side.

2. Facing toward the ceiling and keeping your shoulders as square to the floor as possible, position your hands behind your head. Do not interlace your fingers.

3. Lift your shoulder blades off the floor and exhale as you crunch toward the upturned hip. The range of motion is small—the goal is to lift both shoulders off the floor, but you will not be able to go much farther.

4. Pause at the top position for one second and concentrate on completely contracting the muscles at work. Then lower yourself back to the starting position.

5. Continue crunching until you can no longer lift your shoulders off the floor.

6. Rest for a minute and then perform another set with your opposite hip turned to the floor.

7. Do a second set on each side if you are able.

Lie with knees bent and lowered to one side.

Exhale while crunching toward elevated hip.

Side Hip Raises

This difficult exercise works all the core muscles, and in particular isolates the obliques along the side of your torso.

1. Lie on your side on the floor. Press up with your floor-side arm, keeping it straight and supporting your weight so that your body forms a triangle with the floor. Rest your free arm along the other side of your body.

2. Keeping your supporting arm straight, lower your hip until it touches the floor, then immediately raise it back up to the starting position.

3. Repeat this lowering and raising of the hip in a slow, controlled manner for ten to twenty (hard) repetitions.

4. Rest for one minute and then switch sides to perform another set.

5. Rest for three minutes before performing one more set on each side (if you are able).

Lie on side, tense torso, and support weight with one arm.

Lower hip to floor, then raise.

Lower Back

Often overlooked by conventional training programs, the muscles of the lower back are a common site of weakness and injury among athletes. Fortunately, it takes only a modest commitment of about ten minutes, three days per week, to train these muscles into an asset that will enhance your spinal stability, posture, and performance.

Leg Raise

This is the easiest of the lower-back exercises. Perform this for a few sessions before advancing to the others.

1. Lie facedown on the floor with your legs straight, toes pointed, and arms lying palms-up by your sides. Keep your head in a neutral position with your chin resting lightly on the floor.

2. Contract the muscles of one leg and raise it upward until your foot is 1 to 2 feet off the floor.

3. Pause at the top position for one second, and then lower your leg to the floor.

4. Now contract your other leg and raise it off the floor. Hold the top position for one second and lower this leg to the floor.

5. Continue alternating leg raises for a total of twenty repetitions—but stop sooner than this if you feel any cramping or pain in your lower back.

6. Rest for three minutes, then execute a second set.

Lying facedown, lift one leg . . .

. . . then the other.

Aquaman

The Aquaman, also known as Superhero, is a great core exercise that activates all the muscles between your shoulders and hips.

1. Lie facedown on the floor with your arms extended overhead, your legs straight with pointed toes, and your head in a neutral position.

2. Begin by simultaneously raising one arm and the opposite leg as high as comfortably possible.

3. Hold the top position for one second, then return to the starting position.

4. Repeat by raising the opposite arm and leg off the floor simultaneously. Again hold for a second in the top position before returning to the floor.

5. Continue this alternating exercise motion for a total of twenty repetitions or until you can no longer perform a slow, controlled movement.

6. Rest for three minutes before performing another set, or move on to the next exercise.

Facedown, raise right arm and left leg . . .

. . . then left arm and right leg.

Bruce Lees

This version of a back bridge was a favorite of legendary martial artist Bruce Lee for developing a strong lower back and rock-hard core.

1. Lie on your back with your arms out to the sides, your legs bent at about 90 degrees, and your feet flat on the floor.

2. Press down simultaneously with your feet and shoulders to lift your hips and lower back off the floor. Push your hips toward the ceiling as far as comfortably possible.

3. Hold the top position for one second, then return to the starting position.

4. Continue this motion for ten to twenty reps (hard).

5. Rest for three minutes before performing a second set.

Press down with feet and shoulders . . .

. . . . to lift hips and lower back off floor.

Physioball Exercises

The Physioball, also known as a Swiss ball or exercise ball, is a relative newcomer to sports training, but it does boast some unique benefits. Besides offering a nice change-up to the many floor exercises presented in this chapter, the Physioball's dynamic exercise platform can actually enhance the quality of training. As you use a Physioball, you will discover that more core muscles are called into play in order to maintain stability on the ball throughout each exercise. The Physioball also facilitates some novel core exercises such as the Airplane and Floating Leg Raise.

Ball Crunch

The exercise is very similar to a floor crunch, except that the unstable ball platform causes more core muscles to contract. The ball also allows you to begin the crunch from a slightly hyperextended back position, which increases the range of motion a bit.

1. Lie back on the ball with the middle portion of your back positioned over the top of the ball and your feet firmly planted on the floor about shoulder width apart.

2. Relax your upper torso and neck, and let your head drop slightly below the plane of your body. Place your hands on the back of your head, but do not interlace your fingers.

3. Contract your abdominal muscles and curl your shoulders forward toward your hips until your shoulder blades lift off the ball. Hold this top position for a second, then return to the starting position. Concentrate on exhaling on the way up and inhaling on the way down.

4. Continue this crunch motion until you fatigue or your body position on the ball becomes unstable or slips.

5. Rest for three minutes before performing another set, or move on to the next exercise.

Lie back. Relax upper torso.

Crunch up to lift shoulders off ball.

Floating Leg Raise

This next exercise targets the lower abdominals as you float on your back on top of the ball. This is an excellent supplement to the Ball Crunch—it's also much more difficult!

1. Position the ball 2 to 3 feet from the edge of a heavy bench or chair.

2. Lie back on the ball with middle portion of your back positioned over the top of the ball. Extend your arms behind your head to hold on to the end of the bench. Rest your heels on the floor with slightly bent legs and feet together.

3. Lift your feet off the floor and curl your hips toward your shoulders until your legs approach vertical.

4. Slowly lower your legs toward the floor but stop short of the heels touching; immediately begin the upward phase of the exercise again. Inhale on the way down and exhale on the way up.

5. Continue this motion until your abdominals fatigue or you lose balance on the ball. Move on to the next exercise, or rest for three minutes before performing another set.

Safety note: Maintain just a slight bend in your knees throughout this exercise to reduce stress on your lower back.

Raise legs to near vertical.

Lower to near floor.

Airplane Roll

This exercise improves core balance and control, as well as isolating the oblique muscles on the sides of your torso.

1. Lie on the ball with the middle portion of your back positioned over the top of the ball and your hips off the ball. Plant your feet firmly on the floor, a bit more than shoulder width apart.

2. Extend both arms out to the sides and concentrate on finding a firm, balanced position from which to begin the exercise.

3. Now slowly roll to one side until you can touch your fingertips to the floor. Return to the starting position.

4. Roll in the opposite direction to touch your other hand to the floor.

5. Continue slowly back and forth for ten to twenty repetitions.

6. Rest for three minutes before performing a second set.

Roll left hand to floor.

Then roll right hand to floor.

Bridge

This last exercise is similar to, though much easier than, the Planch move performed by gymnasts. Still, you'll find that it provides a good workout for your shoulders, chest, and back, as well as all the muscles of the core.

1. Assume a push-up position with your arms straight down under your shoulders, your torso straight and in line with your feet, and the top of your feet resting on the top of the ball.

2. Keeping your arms, back, and legs straight, lift one foot off the ball for a few seconds. Contract the muscles of your torso as needed to maintain balance.

3. Return your foot to the ball, then lift the other foot off for a few seconds.

4. Continue lifting one foot at a time off the ball for up to a minute. Stop when you can no longer maintain a straight body position or balance on the ball.

5. Rest for three minutes and execute a second set.

Lift one foot off ball, then the other.

Total Core

These last three core exercises are the most specific and difficult. If you are a novice climber, you should aspire to graduate to these exercises over the course of a few months to a year or two, depending on your initial level of conditioning. Well-conditioned climbers, however, should make these exercises a mainstay of their training program and supplement with a variety of other exercises from earlier in the chapter.

Lift arm and opposite leg, then alternate.

Lifting same-side arm and leg is more difficult.

One-Arm, One-Leg Bridge

This is a surprisingly strenuous exercise and a step up in difficulty from the Physioball Bridge exercise described earlier. It calls into play almost every muscle from your hands to your feet.

1. Assume a push-up position with your torso straight and in line with your feet.

2. Spread your feet shoulder width apart, with your toes in contact with the floor.

3. Keeping your arms, back, and legs straight, lift one foot and the opposite hand off the floor for approximately five seconds. Contract the muscles of your arms, shoulders, core, and legs as needed to maintain balance.

4. Switch foot and arm positions so that your other arm and leg are now supporting your weight. Hold this position for about five seconds.

5. Continue alternating the supporting arm and leg every five seconds. To make the exercise harder, occasionally use the arm and leg on the same side.

6. End the exercise after one minute, or earlier if you cannot maintain balance on the single arm and leg.

7. Rest for three minutes and perform a second set.

Front Lever

Introduced to climbing by the legendary boulderer John Gill, the Front Lever is the gold standard of core-muscle strength. It is a very difficult gymnastics move, so expect this exercise to feel hard—or even impossible! Fortunately, you can make it a bit easier by simply bending one leg or by having a spotter hold your feet.

1. Begin by hanging straight-armed from a bar or a set of pump rocks (harder).

2. Pull up halfway, then push your hands forward, drop your head backward, and lift your legs. Do all this in a single quick motion while attempting to position your entire body—head to toe—parallel to the ground. Squeeze tightly throughout your shoulders, torso, buttocks, and legs to hold this position. It helps to think about pushing your hands toward your hips, even though you'll be in a stationary position.

3. The goal is to hold the lever for two seconds before lowering yourself slowly to the starting position.

4. Immediately pull up into a Front Lever again and hold for two seconds.

5. Perform three to five (hard) total Front Levers.

6. Rest for three to five minutes before performing a second set.

Safety note: The Front Lever places a great deal of stress on your shoulders and elbows (just like steep climbing), so it is inappropriate for novice or out-of-shape climbers or anyone with ongoing elbow or shoulder problems.

Front lever with bent leg.

Front lever with straight legs—harder!

Steep-Wall Traversing

Climbing overhanging walls is the ultimate core-training exercise, and it's obviously the most specific. The best training strategy is to traverse sideways across a long overhanging wall, or back and forth across a shorter one. The only drawback to this exercise is that lack of finger strength and climbing ability will prevent some climbers from traversing long enough to adequately work the core muscles.

1. Select a section of wall that overhangs 20 to 50 degrees past vertical.

2. Using medium-size handholds and small footholds, traverse across the wall at a steady pace. Avoid extremely technical or strenuous moves.

3. Try to make long sideways reaches and stretches with your hands and feet, respectively—the longer the horizontal reaches, the more your core muscles will need to work to maintain balance and stability. Allow your body to twist and turn as needed to execute the moves, and concentrate on contracting your core muscles to prevent body sag, sway, or swing.

4. Continue traversing for at least one minute. Alternate leading with your hands and feet.

5. Rest for three to five minutes before performing a second or third set. Adjust the difficulty of the traverse by using holds that are closer (easier) or farther apart.

The longer the horizontal reach or step, the more effective the core workout.

PHOTO COURTESY OF NICROS, INC. CLIMBING WALLS, WWW.NICROS.COM

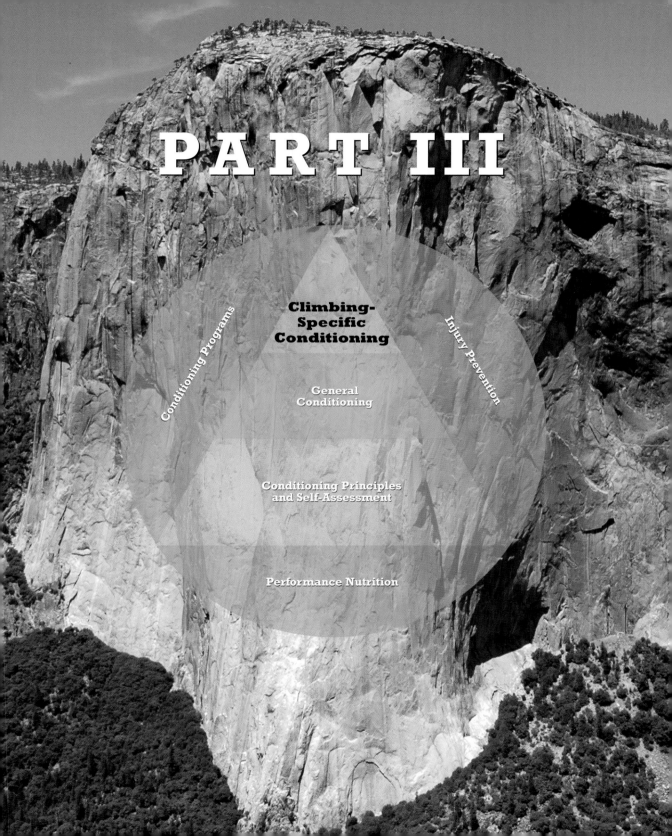

PART III

Climbing-
Specific
Conditioning

Conditioning Programs

Injury Prevention

General
Conditioning

Conditioning Principles
and Self-Assessment

Performance Nutrition

Finger Conditioning

What other sport could possibly ask you to pull your body weight on just a few fingertips? As a result, targeted finger training is uniquely important for climbers.

Perhaps more than any other sport, climbing places extreme demands on your fingers and their controlling muscles in your forearms. Depending on the angle of the rock and size of footholds, your fingers may need to support anywhere from less than 1 percent up to 100 percent of body weight. Compounding these demands is the infinite variety and size of handholds, which can range from a handlebar jug down to a tiny edge or one-finger pocket. What other sport could possibly ask you to pull your body weight on one or two fingertips? This is, of course, an extreme scenario that only elite climbers will encounter; still, the dwindling size of handholds on climbs rated 5.10 and harder does require a level of finger strength not common among flatlanders or novice climbers.

The focus of this chapter is then obvious: to help you strengthen this weakest link to the rock. In your formative days, simply going climbing a few days per week is the only finger training you'll need. As you improve and adapt to the demands of

Cover girl Crystal Norman looking strong at Earth Treks Climbing Center, Timonium, Maryland. PHOTO BY ERIC J. HÖRST

midlevel climbs, however, you'll discover that gains in finger strength and endurance plateau. Breaking through this requires a commitment to targeted training of your fingers.

This chapter provides detailed instruction on two distinct and equally important types of finger conditioning: training your limit strength and training for local endurance. Limit strength is the maximum force you can summon in gripping a small, hard-to-stick hold. Local endurance, however, is the forearm muscle's capability to work at near-maximal intensity for a sustained period, as in climbing a long, overhanging route. In the first section of this chapter, you will learn several cutting-edge strategies for increasing the limit strength of your fingers. Following this, we'll examine several training techniques for increasing local forearm endurance.

Strength-Conditioning Exercises

According to the principle of specificity, efficacy of training to improve grip strength for climbing is proportional to how well it targets the neuromuscular system in ways similar to its use in climbing. For example, squeezing a tennis ball works some of the same muscles used in gripping a climbing handhold; but it does not include the same muscle force, hand and finger position, or energy system used in hard climbing. Therefore, squeezing a tennis ball is ineffective for producing functional grip strength for climbing. Conversely, hanging on a fingerboard or bouldering on small, strenuous-to-grip handholds is very specific and, thus, highly effective training.

The degree to which a given exercise will produce gains in functional grip strength for climbing

Table 6.1 Determining Specificity and Effectiveness of Common Finger Strength Training Exercises

Exercise	High Intensity?	Rapid Failure?	Specific Movement?	Isolate Grips?
Bouldering	yes	maybe	yes	no
Fingerboard	maybe	yes	no	yes
Heavy finger rolls	yes	yes	no	no
One-arm lunging & campus training	yes	yes	sometimes	no
HIT workout	yes	yes	yes	yes

can be estimated by considering the following requirements. The more of these requirements an exercise meets, the more effective it will be at producing gains in usable grip strength.

• **The exercise must be high intensity throughout the entire set.**

In climbing, higher intensity is created by increasing wall angle, decreasing hold size, or increasing hold spacing. Unfortunately, there's a definite limit to how far you can go with each of these. Beyond a certain point, it's more effective to increase intensity by adding weight to your body. Adding just ten pounds can make a huge difference in training intensity on overhanging walls and can yield a leap in finger strength in just a couple of weeks. Interestingly, very few climbers are aware of this fact!

• **The exercise must produce rapid muscular failure, not failure due to poor technique.**

In the weight-lifting world, muscular failure in three to ten reps is considered ideal (though different texts prescribe slightly different values). This is also valid for climbing, but translates to strenuous climbing with failure in six to twenty total hand movements (three to ten moves per hand). In climbing as training, however, there's always the lingering question of whether failure was the result of muscular fatigue or a technical weakness. Thus, the best exercise for training grip strength would reduce the technical requirements as much as possible and

eliminate training of footwork and arm positions.

• **The exercise must be specific to climbing positions and movements.**

The principle of specificity instructs us that strength gains resulting from a certain exercise will be specific to situations involving similar position and movement. The greater the difference between the exercise and the sport use, the less the strength will transfer. Thus, the best grip-strength-training exercises would involve actual climbing movements, whereas an exercise performed while standing or hanging would transfer less.

• **The exercise must focus on a specific grip position for an entire set.**

In climbing, the rock dictates a random use of varying grip positions. Since strength is specific to each grip position, such cycling of grips allows you to climb much longer than you could if you used the same grip repeatedly. That's great if you are climbing for performance; however, it's not ideal for training finger strength. That's why a full season of climbing builds local forearm endurance but may leave you with about the same maximum grip strength as last year. Effective grip-strength training must hammer a specific grip position until failure. Due to the limited transfer of strength among grip positions, you'll need to train several, including open hand, half crimp, full crimp, pinch, and the three two-finger pocket combinations or "teams."

Let's examine five of the more effective exercises for developing functional finger strength. Select two of these exercises for use in every workout session.

Bouldering

Bouldering is the most straightforward way to train grip strength. Without the constraints of a rope and gear, bouldering allows you to focus on climbing the hardest moves possible. Inherent to hard bouldering, however, are some limiting factors that diminish the potential to build maximum grip strength. Consider that technical difficulties may prevent you from climbing up to the point of muscular failure. Furthermore, the rock dictates use of many different grip positions, thus making it difficult to isolate a single grip position and work it to failure.

Despite these limitations, bouldering should be a staple of your training program. It will build some functional strength while at the same time developing mental and technical skills. Consequently, it's a good training strategy to couple bouldering with one of the other finger-strength-training exercises described in the section. Use the following strategy to best stimulate gains in finger strength via bouldering.

1. Select a boulder problem that appears to be strenuous, but not technically difficult. Overhanging problems place more weight on your hands and maximize the training effect. If you are bouldering indoors, try to locate—or consider setting—problems that isolate a specific grip position. For example, a problem that possesses a lot of crimp holds will be best for training crimp strength.

2. Attempt to climb the problem two or three times with sufficient rest between each ascent to allow a good effort. As a guideline, rest for three minutes between attempts of short bouldering problems and five minutes or more between longer problems.

3. Move on to another strenuous-looking problem that appears to target a different grip position, such as pinch, two finger pockets, open hand, and such. Ascend this problem two or three times, with adequate rest between attempts.

4. Continue bouldering for thirty to ninety minutes, and then finish your finger training with one of the isolation exercises described later in the chapter.

Without the constraints of a rope and gear, bouldering allows you to focus on climbing the hardest moves possible.

PHOTO BY ERIC McCALLISTER

Hypergravity Bouldering

Advanced climbers with several years of bouldering under their belt eventually reach a point where they no longer achieve significant gains in finger strength despite regular, hard bouldering. Fortunately, hypergravity bouldering and the HIT workout (described later in this chapter) are powerful training strategies that will yield further gains in high-end finger strength. To do this, you'll need to invest in a ten-pound weight belt or fill a fanny pack with ten pounds of scuba diver's weights. Here is the best strategy for engaging in hypergravity bouldering—this is an indoor training strategy only!

1. Complete a general and sport-specific warm-up. That is, work through various basic stretching exercises, then move on to some general climbing and bouldering for a total of at least twenty to thirty minutes.

2. Clip on your weight belt and predetermine a target number of "burns" (attempts and ascents) that you will perform at hypergravity. As a guideline, limit yourself to about five burns on your initial session, then build to fifteen to twenty burns as you gain confidence and strength.

3. Select nontechnical, overhanging boulder problems that possess small- to medium-size holds, but avoid tiny and tweaky features. Since you are climbing with a weight belt, favor problems below your limit that are strenuous, but doable. It's important to avoid taking an out-of-control fall while climbing with the extra weight on your body.

4. Climb the problem two or three times with sufficient rest between each ascent to allow a good effort. As a guideline, rest for three minutes between attempts of short bouldering problems and five minutes or more between longer problems.

5. Move on to another strenuous-looking problem that appears to target a different grip position. Consider taking the time to set theme problems comprising only holds of a certain shape and size—this is the best way to target and train a weak grip position. Ascend this problem two or three times, with adequate rest between attempts.

Safety notes: Hypergravity bouldering is stressful on the fingers, elbows, and shoulders, and it's critical that you cease this training at the first sign of pain in any of these areas. Gradually work into hypergravity bouldering over the course of a few weeks. Begin with five burns, one day per week, and work toward the advanced program of ten to fifteen burns twice a week.

Bouldering with weight belt.

Fingerboard Repeaters

The fingerboard, also known as a hangboard, is a staple training tool that every serious climber should own. While the large bucket holds on the board can be used for pull-up training, the genius of a good fingerboard is the multitude of finger positions and grips that it enables you to train. This is invaluable if you are unable to regularly boulder or climb. Install a fingerboard in your house and you suddenly have a small piece of "rock" to hang on! Of course, a fingerboard is also a useful tool for supplementing outdoor or wall climbing, since it enables you to target specific grip positions to develop more finger strength.

One caveat: Fingerboard training is not appropriate for a true novice or anyone with recent incidence of a finger, elbow, or shoulder injury. As a guideline, you can begin fingerboard training if you've been climbing for more than six months, you are not more than a few pounds overweight, and you have no ongoing pain in the fingers, arms, or shoulders. A final rule of fingerboard training is to never use the board more than three days per week.

Repeaters are the best fingerboard exercise for developing maximum grip strength, since they target specific grip positions with repeated high-intensity contractions. Before you get started, however, it's imperative that you perform a complete warm-up—lest your fingerboard become the "injury board." Don't take chances; use the warm-up exercises detailed in chapter 3. Also consider reinforcing the tendons at the base of your fingers with a few tight turns of tape (see page 98).

1. Since you will be hanging with both hands gripping a pair of identical holds, survey your fingerboard to identify the grips you can use. Select five to ten grip positions to be trained; for example,

open hand, pinch, crimp, sloper, three-finger pocket, and various two-finger pocket combinations. Begin by training your weakest grip position—the one that is most difficult to use when climbing—and end with your strongest. (See table 6.2)

2. Execute one set of ten Repeaters. Each hang should last just three to five seconds, with a rest between hangs of less than five seconds. To be effective, the hangs must be high intensity and require that you bear down hard to maintain the grip for a three- to five-second count (count *one thousand one, one thousand two,* and so on). You may need to add anywhere from five to twenty pounds of weight around your waist (hypergravity training) to make the task this difficult. It may take you a few sessions to determine the exact amount of weight needed for a specific grip position. Use a smaller fingerboard feature if you need more than twenty pounds to make this exercise difficult.

3. After completing a full set of Repeaters, take a three- to five-minute rest. Perform light stretching or self-massage during this recovery period.

4. Select a different pair of holds and begin a second set of Repeaters. Use the exact protocol described in step 2. You may need a different amount of weight around your waist for this new grip position.

5. Rest again for three to five minutes, then begin a third set of Repeaters using a different set of holds.

6. Continue alternating sets of Repeaters with rest periods for a total of five to ten sets.

The fingerboard.

Table 6.2 Sample Fingerboard Repeater Workout

Grip Position	Reps/Hangs	Weight Added (lbs.)	Rest before Next Set or Grip Position (minutes)
Pinch	10	0	3
Open-hand "sloper"	10	0	3
Two-Finger pocket (pinkie/ring)	10	0	3
Two-Finger pocket (index/middle)	10	10	3
Two-Finger pocket (middle/ring)	10	10	3
Small crimp	10	10	3
Three-Finger pocket (all but pinkie)	10	20	3
Medium crimp	10	20	3

Heavy Finger Rolls

What this exercise lacks in specificity to climbing, it makes up for in high-intensity neuromuscular stimulation. Perhaps more than any other exercise, Heavy Finger Rolls produce noticeable hypertrophy (an increase in the size of muscle cells) and quantifiable gains in finger strength. Therefore, tremendous training synergy can result from coupling Heavy Finger Rolls with a climbing-specific exercise such as bouldering or fingerboard repeaters.

One barrier to engaging in Heavy Finger Roll training is finding the necessary weight-training equipment. You will need access to a 200-pound free-weight set, a bench press bar with ball-bearing sleeves, and a squat rack. If you belong to a traditional health club or well-equipped climbing gym, then you are in luck. Otherwise, you'll need to determine whether training with this exercise is worth the significant investment in equipment (around $500)—although it will also come in handy for antagonist muscle conditioning.

1. First, you need to set up the equipment to facilitate training with heavy weights. Set the squat rack so that the bench-press bar rests at about knee height. Load weight plates onto the bar to a warm-up weight equal to about half your body weight.

2. Stand in the middle of the squat rack and grip the bar with your hands shoulder width apart and thumbs pointing outward. Now lift the bar to gain the exercise stance with the bar lightly touching your thighs. Body position is critical to reduce strain on your lower back, elbows, and wrists—bend slightly at your knees, center your hips and shoulders over your feet, and maintain

Stand with hips and shoulders over feet, with a slight bend in arms and knees, and a straight lower back.

Roll bar from open-hand position . . .

. . . to closed-hand position.

good posture with your lower back straight and head up. It helps to perform this exercise standing in front of a mirror, so you can monitor your technique while looking straight ahead.

3. Begin rolling the bar up and down in your fingers. The range of motion is only the few inches from the open-hand position to the closed-hand position. Ideally you want to lower the bar as far as possible without it falling from your hand. The squat rack is your spotter just in case the bar does slip from your fingers. Maintain a still, stable body position throughout the exercise—do not jerk the weight with your arms in an attempt to perform extra reps.

4. Continue rolling the bar up and down for a total of ten to twenty warm-up reps, and then replace the bar on the rack.

5. Rest for three to five minutes, then move on to the first of five training sets. (See table 6.3)

6. Your training weight must be heavy in order to be effective. Use body weight as a starting value, but increase the weight as needed to produce failure in five to ten repetitions. Well-trained individuals may need to use as much as 150 percent of body weight. Rest three to five minutes between sets.

Safety notes: Maintaining proper form is critical—cease this exercise if you experience pain in your knees, lower back, shoulders, elbows, wrist, or fingers. Use of supportive tape for the A2 pulley of your middle and ring fingers is strongly encouraged.

Training notes: Cycle on and off of this exercise every few weeks. Heavy Finger Rolls are best used in the maximum-strength phase of a training cycle.

Table 6.3 Sample Heavy Finger Roll Workout for a 160-Pound Climber			
Set	Weight	Reps	Rest between Sets (minutes)
Warm-up	95	15–20	3–5
1	155	10–12	3–5
2	185	10–12	3–5
3	195	5–10	3–5
4	205	3–5	3–5
5	205	3–5	3–5

One-Arm Traversing

One-arm traversing is a simple exercise with two big payoffs: increased grip strength and better speed of contraction (contact strength). Contact strength is a function of how fast muscular motor units can be called into play—this determines how fast you can summon maximum grip strength on a small hold. Use this exercise twice per week as a complement to high-intensity training such as hypergravity bouldering, Heavy Finger Rolls, and such.

1. Select a vertical section of an indoor wall with enough room to traverse 10 to 20 feet on medium- to large-size handholds and small- to medium-size footholds.

2. Climb up onto the wall so that your feet are just a foot or two off the floor. Now, remove one hand from the wall and hold it behind your back. Begin traversing with small, quick lunges from one handhold to the next. Advance your feet to new footholds as needed to keep your center of gravity over your feet and maintain balance.

3. Continue traversing for eight to twelve total hand moves, and then step off the wall.

4. After a brief rest, step back up onto the wall and traverse the opposite direct using your other hand.

5. Perform two or three one-arm traverses with each hand.

Safety notes: It's important to perform small, controlled lunges that allow you to catch the next hold with a slight bend in your elbow. Shoulder and elbow injuries could result from consistently catching lunges with a fully extended arm or shoulder. Stop this exercise if you feel pain in your fingers, elbows, or shoulders.

Traverse a vertical wall with one hand. Move in the direction of the arm in use.

One-Arm Lunging

Once you are proficient at one-arm traversing on vertical walls, you can proceed to one-arm up-and-down lunges on a slightly overhanging wall. This exercise is also done "feet on," but the steeper angle creates greater dynamic force, especially on the downward catch. This extra stress will trigger further neuromuscular adaptations, and it's a good icebreaker before graduating to the campus training exercises described in chapter 7.

1. Select a section of indoor wall that overhangs anywhere from 5 to 25 degrees past vertical—the steeper the wall, the more difficult the exercise—and possesses numerous medium-size hand- and footholds. Ideally, you can set a few modular holds specifically for One-Arm Lunging. Set two footholds about a foot off the ground, and then set two non-tweaky medium-size handholds, one in front of your face and the other about 2 feet above that.

2. Climb onto the wall and balance your weight evenly on the two footholds. Grip the hold in front of your face with one hand, then let go with the other hand and hold it behind your back.

3. Begin lunging up and down between the two handholds in a manner similar to the One-Arm Traversing exercise discussed previously. Optimal technique is to draw your body toward the wall and lunge up to the top hold, doing so all in one smooth motion. This drawing-in of the body facilitates a quick grab at the next hold while upward momentum briefly reduces your load—this is commonly called a deadpoint move. Upon catching the top handhold, immediately drop back down to the starting hold and, without pause, explode back up to the top hold.

4. Continue lunging up and down for eight to twelve total hand movements, then step down off the wall.

5. After a brief rest, step back up on the wall and perform a set of One-Arm Lunges with your other hand.

6. Perform two or three total sets with each hand.

Safety note: This exercise dynamically loads all components of the fingers and arms. Proceed with caution, and cease the exercise if you experience any joint or tendon pain.

Balance weight evenly on two good footholds.

Lunge one-handed between two handholds.

Taping to Reinforce Tendons

Circumferential taping at the base of the fingers has been shown to slightly reduce the stress placed on the finger tendon pulleys. Although I do not advocate the use of taping all the time, it is a good practice if you are recovering from a tendon injury or engaging in a stressful climb or exercise, such as fingerboard, hypergravity, and campus training. The A2 ring method is more common, but the X method is useful for protecting the skin during hypergravity training or on high-volume climbing days. Most people tape only the middle and ring fingers, since these are the most commonly injured fingers.

- ■ **A2 Ring.** Wrap three firm turns of tape around the base of the finger. Apply the tape as tightly as possible without restricting blood flow.

- ■ **X Method.** Tear a strip of tape approximately 16 inches long by 0.75 inch wide. With a slight bend in the finger, begin with two turns of tape around the base. Continue over the palm side of the lower finger joint, taking two turns around the middle finger bone. Cross back over the palm side of the lower finger joint and conclude with another full turn around the base of the finger.

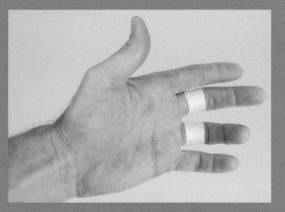

A2 ring.

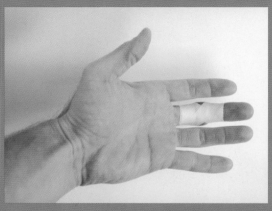

X Method.

Hypergravity Isolation Training

I developed Hypergravity Isolation Training (HIT) in the mid-1990s, and it has since been adopted by thousands of climbers around the world as their top choice for training maximum finger strength. Not to be confused with the "HIT" program used by bodybuilders, this highly specific grip-training method involves adding weight to your body (to simulate hypergravity) and then climbing on identical finger holds to isolate a specific grip position to failure. HIT meets the four fundamental requisites for training

maximum grip strength (described earlier in the chapter), and it is in fact the gold standard for training finger strength.

In the photo (opposite) you see me training on third-generation HIT Strips (available from Nicros, Inc.), a unique platform I develop for optimal HIT workouts. Each HIT Strip possesses identical crimp edges and two-finger pockets, so that I can "ladder" up and down until failure. I increase or decrease the weight added around my waist to produce grip failure in twenty or fewer total hand movements (ten

The author training two-finger pocket strength on the HIT system. Note the 20-pound belts around his waist.

or fewer per hand). My feet simply step on resident holds on the wall so my body can turn as it would in climbing a steep route. This is obviously an extremely specific exercise that targets— indeed, hammers!—all the major grip positions used in climbing. For intermediate and advanced climbers, there is simply no better way to train grip strength.

■ WALL SETUP

Use an overhanging bouldering wall of 0.75-inch plywood at an angle of 45 to 55 degrees past vertical. HIT workouts on a 55-degree (past vertical) wall are significantly harder than those on the common 45-degree wall. If you are building a wall for HIT workouts, I advise a compromise angle of 50 degrees. Wall angles overhanging less than 45 degrees or more than 55 degrees are not appropriate for HIT workouts.

Sitting on the floor under the wall, mount the first HIT Strip at top-of-head height. Mount four more strips at 18- to 20-inch intervals. Two pinch holds are positioned above the first HIT Strip at shoulder width. The remaining pinch holds are mounted above the other HIT Strips at similar intervals.

Alternatively, you can rig a HIT-type setup using modular holds. You will need, however, ten identical two-finger pocket holds, ten identical crimp holds, and ten identical pinch holds that are all usable on a 50-degree overhanging wall. If you don't have these holds, it may be cheaper and certainly more advantageous to invest in the HIT Strip system (which runs $195–$250). Training on HIT Strips will help you maintain focus on the goal of using only the specific grip being trained, whereas using modular holds may lead you into breaking the sequence when you get pumped as you stray onto other modular holds. Furthermore, the HIT Strips are optimized for a 50-degree wall and possess a safe, ergonomic radius of curvature to lower the pain factor when you're climbing with weight.

Table 6.4 Sample HIT Workouts

Grip Position and Set	Weight to Add—Novice* (pounds)	Weight to Add—Expert* (pounds)	Reps per Set**	Rest between Sets (minutes)
Pinch	0	20	<20	3
Two-Finger third team	0	20	<20	3
Two-Finger second team	10	40	<20	3
Two-Finger first team	10	40	<20	3
Full crimp	10	40	<20	3
Half crimp	10	40	<20	3

* Weights are approximations for a 160-pound climber. Use similar percentages of your body weight if it's much different.

** After a few cycles of HIT, you may want to execute two sets using each grip position.

The HIT workout trains six basic grip positions, beginning with your weakest grip position and concluding with your strongest. For most people the training order will be pinch grip, two-finger "third team" (pinkie and ring finger), two-finger "second team" (index and middle finger), two-finger "first team" (middle and ring finger), full crimp, and half crimp.

1. Sit on the floor below the first HIT Strip, and then grab onto the lowest pair of pinch holds.

Pull up and grab the next higher left-hand pinch hold. Adjust your feet as needed, then upgrade your right hand to the next pinch hold (third level). Continue up the pinch holds until both hands are grasping the top pair of pinches.

2. Immediately begin reversing the sequence by alternating left and right pinch holds to descend the wall. Again, your feet can use any footholds and your body can turn naturally to provide optimal position and tension for each hand move.

HIT Workout Tips

- Always engage in an extended period of warm-up activities and bouldering before beginning a HIT workout.

- Limit your total hand moves per set to twenty or fewer (ten or fewer per hand) by adding weight around your waist. Purchase one or more 10-pound weight belts or, alternatively, place several scuba diver's weights into a fanny pack. Do not use a weighted backpack—this weight would be cumbersome and unnatural due to its displacement from your center of gravity.

- Climb briskly and without hesitation—do not stop or pause midset to rest or chalk up. Consider using a spotter so that you can climb confidently up to the point of failure.

- Try to climb through the reps with normal foot movements and body turns. Smaller foot holds (about an inch deep) are better, yet giving too much thought to footwork will slow you down—the goal is to train your fingers, not footwork and technique.

- Limit rests between sets to exactly three minutes. Use a stopwatch and stick to the planned order and schedule of exercises. Only this way will you be able to quantify and track your gains in finger strength! If you're sloppy on the length of rests, the numbers become meaningless.

- Keep a training book in which you log the weight added and reps performed for each set. Then you'll always know what weight you need for a given set and can easily track your gains (weight and rep increases) from workout to workout.

- Always do your HIT workout in the same order, and never perform more than two sets per grip position! Performing a third set will provide little added stimulus, but it will dig a deeper hole for you to recover from (requiring more days) and add to your risk of injury.

- Tape your fingers to help protect your tendons and increase the skin comfort.

- Sand down the HIT Strips slightly if the texture causes pain that prevents you from completing each set to muscular failure.

- Increase rest days if you find your HIT reps and weights decreasing. If you ever feel weak on the rock after a HIT workout, it's due to insufficient rest—it can take up to three to five days to recover from a HIT workout. Expect initial workouts to require a longer recovery period, whereas your future adaptations will speed recovery to just two or three days.

- Cycle on and off HIT every two weeks, or employ HIT workouts during the three-week maximum-strength phase of the 4-3-2-1 or 3-2-1 Training Cycles (see chapter 10).

3. Upon reaching the starting pinch holds, immediately start back up the wall using only alternating pinch handholds. Continue up and down the wall until your pinch grip fails.

4. Upon stepping off the wall, use a stopwatch to time a rest of exactly three minutes before beginning the next set. Meanwhile, record the total number of hand movements (or reps) in your training notebook.

5. If you were able to do twenty or more hand moves, then you must add weight when training the pinch grip in the future. Add 5 pounds if you just barely succeeded at climbing twenty hand movements; add 10 pounds if the twenty hand movements felt easy. Note that doing more than twenty reps (ten movements per hand) will train anaerobic endurance, while adding weight to produce failure in ten or fewer reps per hand trains maximum grip strength, which is of course our goal here.

6. After your three-minute rest, proceed immediately with your next set on the HIT Strips. Advanced climbers with experience at HIT should perform a second set of the pinch grip, while those new to the workout should move on to the next grip position.

7. Continue alternating training burns with rests of exactly three minutes until you have worked through all the grip positions. Always record the number of hand movements performed as well as the amount of weight added for each grip position. This data will be helpful in doing future HIT workouts, and it will quantify—finally—that your finger strength is indeed increasing!

Safety notes: Tape your middle and ring fingers using the X method shown on page 98. This is imperative when training with 20 or more pounds added to your body. End your HIT workout early if you experience any pain in the joints or tendons of the fingers or arms.

Local Endurance-Conditioning Exercises

Endurance local to the forearm muscles—physiologically a matter of anaerobic endurance—is what enables you to hang on and pull through many hard moves in a row. (Many climbers refer to anaerobic endurance with the pseudo term *power endurance*.) Your ability to persevere through a long sequence of strenuous moves, despite a growing forearm pump, is a function of the mind and body's tolerance to the fatiguing effects of blood lactate and other metabolic by-products, and your body's ability to remove these by-products from the working muscles. Central to this removal process is the density of the capillary network that innervates the forearm muscles—the more capillaries that are present and the larger their diameter, the faster lactic acid can be cleared from the muscle. Interestingly, increasing your limit strength will also yield a modest increase in local endurance—so training to increase maximum strength will also produce some improvement in muscular endurance! Therefore, a well-designed program will include training exercises for both limit strength and local endurance. Or you can cycle back and forth between these two different—but equally important—types of training.

As stated earlier, simply climbing a few days per week is moderately effective for building local endurance. A few of the more popular strategies are climbing laps on routes, interval training on boulder problems, and performing long traverses. As long as your climbing activities are producing a muscular burn and "pump," you can rest assured that your body will adapt favorably to your training.

Let's look at four exercises that target the forearm muscles in the quest for more endurance of finger strength. Chapter 7 will provide additional instruction on developing anaerobic endurance in the larger pull muscles of your upper body.

Light Finger Rolls

This is the least specific of all the endurance-training exercises, but it's good for a warm-up or if you don't have access to the equipment necessary for the other exercises. As opposed to the strength-building Heavy Finger Rolls described earlier, training endurance with these rolls requires a much lighter weight and higher number of repetitions. Follow the guidelines below and you will get a good forearm pump!

1. Use a dumbbell that weighs about 20 percent of your total body weight.

2. Sit on a bench with your feet about shoulder width apart and firmly planted on the floor.

3. Position the arm to be trained between your legs with the palm facing outward and the back of your forearm resting on your leg.

4. Begin rolling the dumbbell up and down in your fingers. The range of motion is only the few inches from the open-hand position to the closed-hand position. Ideally, you want to lower the dumbbell as far as possible without it falling from your hand.

5. Continue rolling the dumbbell up and down for a total of forty to sixty repetitions. Use a lighter weight if you cannot complete at least forty reps.

6. Now perform forty to sixty reps with the other hand.

7. Execute a second and third set with each hand. Take no rest between sets other than the rest each arm gets while the other is training.

Training note: This high-volume, short-rest training strategy should produce a significant forearm pump. If not, increase the weight by 5 to 10 pounds for your next workout.

Roll dumbbell from open-hand position . . .

. . . to closed-hand position.

Figure 6.1 Fingerboard Pyramid Training

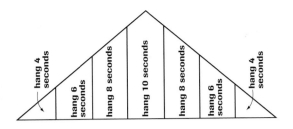

(hang 4 seconds · hang 6 seconds · hang 8 seconds · hang 10 seconds · hang 8 seconds · hang 6 seconds · hang 4 seconds)

Fingerboard Pyramids

Pyramid training simulates the way your forearm muscles might work in climbing a medium-length gym route. As shown in figure 6.1, one run through the Fingerboard Training Pyramid involves seven hangs on the same pair of holds. After a brief rest, you will perform another pyramid cycle on a different set of holds. Continuing in this interval-training fashion, you can work all the primary grip positions over the course of seven to fifteen total sets. This is an excellent routine for developing local forearm endurance.

1. As with all finger-training exercises, it's vital that you begin by engaging in a progressive warm-up of light exercise, stretching, and then moderate climbing or a few sets of hangs and pull-ups.

2. Begin your pyramid training by targeting your weakest grip position. For many people, this will be the sloper or pinch grip.

3. Follow the pyramid exactly with only a five-second rest between each hang. It's best to sub-vocalize a slow count of *one thousand one, one thousand two,* and so on. The first full pyramid will take just under one and a half minutes.

4. Take a one-minute rest before performing another pyramid cycle on a different set of holds.

5. Repeat this cycle for a total of seven to fifteen sets. Work a different grip position with each set;

however, do stick to a single grip for each pass through the pyramid cycle.

Safety notes: Consider taping your middle fingers with the A2 method shown on page 98. Terminate your pyramid training early if you feel any pain in your tendons or joints.

Fingerboard Moving Hangs

Moving hangs involve working your hands around the board continuously for several minutes, much like climbing a long sustained sequence on the rock. Doing this requires somewhere to place your feet while your hands switch holds on the board. The best way to do this is to mount your fingerboard so that it's set out a foot or two from a wall onto which you have mounted a few small footholds or other foot support. Another possibility is to mount the board above a doorway, then position a chair or stool a couple feet behind the board. Either way, you will be able to use your toes for support as you circulate your hands around the fingerboard.

1. Perform a twenty to thirty-minute warm-up comprising some aerobic activity, stretching, and some pull-ups and easy hangs on the fingerboard. You should break a light sweat and feel a slight pump in your arms.

2. Mount the board, then place your feet on footholds or on the edge of a chair.

3. Begin moving your hands around the fingerboard, changing hand positions every three to five seconds.

4. After a minute or two, you will begin to develop a pump in your forearms. Move both hands onto the largest handholds on the board, and shake out each arm for about thirty seconds in an attempt to recover a little.

5. After this brief shakeout, continue moving your hands around the board for another minute or two. Once again, move to the large holds if you need to shake out and rest your muscles a little.

6. Continue in this fashion with the goal of staying on the board for a total of five to ten minutes.

7. Dismount the board, and rest for about ten minutes before proceeding with a second and third set.

HIT or System Training Body-Weight Laps

The HIT Strip platform or a specialized System Wall can also be used to train anaerobic endurance via an interval-training strategy. This requires an approach that's completely different from the HIT maximum-strength workout described earlier. The goal now is to climb thirty to sixty total hand moves with only brief rest periods and no weight added to your body. For most climbers, it will be impossible to climb enough hand movements using the weaker pinch and two-finger pocket third team. Therefore, I suggest you train two different general finger positions: two-finger pocket (in which you cycle through all three two-finger teams) and crimp (in which you alternate full and half crimp as you climb). Train two-finger pocket endurance first.

1. Sit on the floor below the first HIT Strip or pair of System Holds, and then grab on to the lowest pair of pocket holds using the two-finger third team.

2. Begin laddering upward by grabbing alternating strips with the left and right hand. Upon reaching the top HIT Strip, immediately reverse the sequence back down the wall. Climb with open feet (use any footholds you like) and allow your body to naturally twist and turn to provide optimal position.

3. Use the two-finger pocket third team for as many hand moves as possible, then switch to the second team, and finally the first team.

4. Continue laddering up and down for between thirty to sixty total hand moves.

5. Rest for just one to two minutes, then commence with a high-rep set using just the full- and half-crimp grips. Again, strive for a total of thirty to sixty repetitions.

6. Upon completing the two sets, take a five-minute rest.

Fingerboard Moving Hangs: Change hand positions every few seconds, while maintaining one or two feet on footholds.

7. Consider repeating the above sequence one or two more times. This should result in a deep pump and muscle burn—a highly specific and effective local endurance workout!

Safety notes: Consider X-taping your middle and ring fingers (see page 98) so that you won't have to stop prematurely due to skin pain. Do stop, however, if you experience any pain in your finger joints or tendons.

The Tabata Protocol

The Tabata Protocol is not an exercise per se, but instead a highly specific method of interval training that can be applied to a wide variety of exercises and activities. Developed by Japanese fitness researcher Izumi Tabata, the Tabata couples a twenty-second-maximum intensity period of exercise with a ten-second rest interval. This work-rest couplet is repeated up to eight times before any additional rest is taken—the result is four minutes of heart-pumping, muscle-burning exercise.

The Tabata protocol differs from traditional interval training methods in three ways: The work interval is more intense (greater exercise speed or resistance), the work interval is shorter, and the rest interval is so brief that very little recovery can occur before the next work interval begins. Research has shown the Tabata protocol to provide greater gains in anaerobic capacity (as well as measurable gains in aerobic capacity) compared to traditional interval training, although longer rest intervals are superior for training anaerobic recovery (removal of lactic acid and other metabolic by-products). Consequently, climbers can benefit from use of both the Tabata protocol and the traditional interval-training methods.

Following is one application of the Tabata Protocol for training anaerobic endurance of the forearm muscles on the HIT System. However, you can apply this same training strategy to other exercises such as Light Finger Rolls, Fingerboard Hangs, and Lat Pull-Downs, as well as to a variety of less specific free-weight and aerobic exercises.

1. Sit on the floor below the first HIT Strip, then grab onto the lowest HIT Strip using either the two-finger pocket or crimp-grip holds.

2. Begin the first twenty-second work interval by briskly laddering up and down using alternating HIT strips. Most climbers achieve about fifteen hand moves (1.5 laps on the strips) in twenty seconds; you'll need to determine exactly how many hand moves you can do in twenty seconds.

3. Rest for exactly ten seconds, then resume climbing up and down the HIT Strips for another twenty seconds. Climb with open feet (use any footholds you like), and allow your body to naturally twist and turn to provide optimal body position.

4. Rest again for exactly ten seconds, and then begin your third twenty-second climbing interval.

5. Continue for six to eight total intervals, which will take three or four minutes, respectively.

6. Rest for five minutes, before you ponder a second HIT System Tabata!

Training notes: The efficacy of the Tabata depends on precise work and rest intervals and near maximum exertion. Stick to the schedule exactly—the ten-second rest is barely enough to quickly rechalk your hands and reposition below the first HIT Strip. Similarly, the climbing intervals should be intense and exactly twenty seconds in length. If you aren't exhausted and gasping for breath by the seventh and eighth intervals, then you need to add a 10- or 20-pound weight belt for future sessions. Finally, vary the grip position you use every set (alternate between two-finger pocket and crimp grip) to help you persevere through the Tabata, and consider taping your fingers to limit skin wear and pain. Do no more than two Tabata sequences per workout, and limit use of Tabata to just two days per week.

The HIT Tabata: Ladder up and down HIT strips using the two-finger pocket or crimp grip.

Upper-Body Strength, Power, and Endurance Conditioning

A training-for-climbing program will be most effective only if it addresses your greatest weakness, whether it is physical, mental, or technical.

Although your fingers and toes are your primary link to the rock, it's the larger muscles of your arms, legs, and torso that facilitate most of the upward movement in climbing. Of course, lack of leg strength is rarely, if ever, a limiting constraint on the rock—it's the large pull muscles of the upper body that are most likely to fail you. Therefore, developing more upper-body strength, power, and endurance must be central to every training-for-climbing program.

Most important to climbers are the large muscles of the upper arm, shoulders, and back, including the biceps, deltoids, rhomboids, trapezius, and lats. There are many other muscles throughout the chest and abdomen that come into play as well; however, the focus of the exercises in this chapter are the workhorse pull muscles that are vital to upward movement and sustaining lock-off positions. In properly targeting these larger muscles, it is important to reduce the demands on the smaller forearm muscles so that they are not a limiting factor in training the process. By principle, specific fin-

ger and forearm training (as detailed in the chapter 6) should be a distinctly separate activity that's completed *before* engaging in targeted training of the larger pull muscles.

This chapter is divided into three sections that provide specific exercises for developing limit strength, power, and anaerobic endurance. Although an exercise from one section may resemble an exercise in another section, closer study will reveal very different protocols for training strength versus power or endurance. Each of these capabilities is physiologically different, and therefore effective training of each requires a different strategy. In putting these exercises to use, it's best to focus on a single goal for a given workout—to train strength, power, or endurance—instead of trying to train all three in a single session. Chapter 10 will then provide sample training programs and guidelines for varying your training focus to achieve optimal results in each area.

Strength-Conditioning Exercises

Training limit strength requires high exercise loads that will produce muscular failure in ten repetitions or less. The upcoming five exercises all meet these criteria, assuming you follow the directions precisely. In some cases you'll need to wear one or more weight belts (hypergravity training) to create the necessary training load. Other exercises require specialized equipment such as a campus board or the pull-down machine. Regardless of how many of these exercises are available to you, it's best to select just one or two for use in any given limit-strength workout.

Jonathan Manz on **Fear and Loathing** *(5.12a),*
Red Rocks, Nevada. PHOTO BY ERIC J. HÖRST

Weighted Pull-Ups

As introduced in chapter 6, hypergravity training is also a useful workout strategy for developing limit strength in the pull muscles. Weighted Pull-Ups are the simplest way to get started. Wearing a 10-pound weight belt (or more) while doing your pull-up training will trigger the neuromuscular system to adapt to your higher apparent body weight. Upon returning to the rock to climb at body weight, you will feel noticeably lighter and climb stronger given this newfound überstrength. Here's how to do it.

1. Attach a 10-pound weight belt around your waist. Extremely fit individuals may need to use two or three 10-pound belts or even a 40- or 50-pound weight vest.

2. Grip a pull-up bar in the palms-away position or use the largest holds on a fingerboard. Your hands should be about shoulder width apart.

3. Pull up at a relatively fast rate in order to reach the top position in one second or less. Pause at the top position for just a moment, and then lower to a two-second count. Subvocalize, *one thousand one, one thousand two.*

4. Upon reaching the bottom position, immediately begin your next pull-up.

5. Continue in this fashion until you can no longer perform a complete pull-up.

6. Perform two to four sets with a rest interval of at least three minutes between sets.

7. Increase the weight added by 10 pounds when you are able to do four sets of ten repetitions.

Safety notes: Do not hang in the straight-armed position to rest between repetitions—this is extremely stressful on the shoulders. Stop doing Weighted Pull-Ups if you sense any unusual pain in your shoulders or elbow.

Heavy Pull-Downs

Health clubs and some climbing gyms possess a pull-down machine that can be used in place of the Weighted Pull-Ups exercise described above. This is the one machine exercise that climbers can perform using a heavy training load; in fact, you want to use a weight heavy enough to produce failure in five to ten total repetitions.

1. Adjust the seat and knee lock so that you grasp the pull-down bar with arms fully extended.

2. Grip the bar with your hands shoulder width apart. Many pull-down machines possess bars designed for the much wider hand position preferred by bodybuilders—do not use this wide grip! It's okay to occasionally use a narrow grip.

3. Pull the bar down below your chin and ideally until it touches your upper chest. Pause and hold the bar to your chest for one second, and then release the bar to a two-second count. Subvocalize, *one thousand one, one thousand two.*

4. Upon reaching the starting, straight-armed position, immediately begin your next pull-down.

5. Continue in this fashion until you can no longer pull the bar to touch your upper chest.

6. Perform two to four sets with a rest interval of at least three minutes between sets.

7. If you are able to do more than ten repetitions, you should increase the weight by 10 pounds for your next set.

Safety notes: Do not pull the bar behind your head, as some health club programs suggest; this is unnecessarily stressful and potentially injurious to the shoulders. Terminate this exercise if you sense any unusual pain in your shoulders.

Weighted Pull-Ups: Wearing a weight belt or weight vest, grip large handholds and pull up.

Uneven-Grip Pull-Ups

This is an excellent exercise for developing one-arm strength and lock-off ability. Train with Uneven Grip Pull-Ups long enough and you'll eventually develop the rare ability to do a one-arm pull-up. This exercise requires a setup that offsets one hand 12 to 24 inches lower than the other. You can loop a sling over a pull-up bar or extend one of a pair of free-floating Pump Rocks.

1. Begin with your hands offset vertically by about 18 inches.

2. Pull up with a focus on pulling hardest with your high hand. As you ascend to the height of the lower hand, begin pushing downward with the lower hand, if needed, to aid further upward motion.

3. Continue to pull up with the high hand until it is drawn in tight against the front of your shoulder.

4. Lower yourself to the starting position to a two-second count, then immediately begin the next repetition.

5. Continue in this manner until you can no longer pull up the whole way with your high hand.

6. Rest for a minute or two, and then switch hands to train the opposite side.

7. Perform two or three sets on each side with the goal of five to ten repetitions per set. Increase the vertical distance between your hands if you can do more than ten reps; decrease the distance if you cannot do at least five repetitions.

Uneven-Grip Pull-Ups: Pull up with both hands, pulling hardest with high hand.

Hold lock-off for a moment, then lower.

One-Arm Lock-Off

The ability to hold a steady one-arm lock-off is vital for hard bouldering and roped climbing. This exercise is obviously very specific to this need—but it does demand a high level of base strength for proper execution. If you cannot do twenty pull-ups, it would be best to train with Weighted or Uneven-Grip Pull-Ups instead of this exercise.

1. Begin with both hands grasping the top of a single Pump Rock. For example, if you plan to lock-off on the right arm, you'd place your left hand on top of your right—but with your left hand grabbing from the opposite side of the Pump Rock. Using a pull-up bar, position your hands side by side, with palms facing each other.

2. Pull up into the lock-off position, and then immediately let go with the top hand (in this case the left). Hold the static lock-off position as long as possible, ideally for between ten and twenty seconds (hard). It helps to think about pulling the Pump Rock toward your armpit.

3. When you begin to lose the lock-off, either grab back on with the other hand or lower yourself slowly to the straight-armed position. Do not drop yourself rapidly into the straight-armed position!

4. Dismount and rest for one minute before executing a one-arm lock-off in the same fashion with the other arm.

5. After executing one lock-off with each arm, take a three-minute rest before performing another one-arm lock with each arm.

One-Arm Lock-Off: Pull up with both hands, let one hand go, hold in static one-arm lock-off position.

6. Do a total of two to four lock-offs with each hand.

Safety notes: Doing this exercise on a free-hanging set of Pump Rocks is much less stressful on your elbows and shoulders (and a bit easier) than attempting to do them on a fixed apparatus such as a pull-up bar or fingerboard. Regardless of the training platform, stop doing One-Arm Lock-Offs if you experience any pain in your elbows or shoulders.

Campus Lock-Offs

Campus Lock-Offs, also known as Campus Touches, train the dynamic lock-off ability that's often called on for making a long reach on steep climbing terrain. This is an excellent exercise to couple with one of the previous lock-off exercises or with the Weighted Pull-Ups or Heavy Pull-Downs. Training with Campus Lock-Offs requires a unique campus board consisting of a slightly overhanging wall equipped with specialized Campus Strips (visit TrainingForClimbing.com to learn about building a campus board).

1. Begin by hanging with both hands from a low rung on the board.

2. Pull up forcefully with both hands, then in a fast, continuous motion, lunge up with one hand to grab the highest rung possible (usually the third or fourth rung, depending on the spacing).

3. Engage the high rung for an instant, and then

Campus Lock-Offs:
Hang from a low rung with both hands.

Pull up with both hands, then lunge with left hand and grab high rung for an instant.

drop back down to the starting hold and lower to the starting (hanging) position.

4. Immediately pull back up and lunge with the opposite hand to grab a high rung.

5. Again, engage the high rung for a moment before dropping down to the starting hold and lowering to your starting position.

6. Continue in this alternating fashion for up to twelve total touches (six per hand).

7. Rest for three to five minutes before performing another set. Do two to four sets.

Safety note: Cease Campus Lock-Offs if you feel joint or tendon pain in your fingers, arms, or shoulders.

Training note: You can make this exercise harder by touching, but not grabbing on to, the high hold at the top of each lunge. Try to hold the lock-off and touch for two seconds.

Drop down to bottom rung and regrip with both hands.

Pull up with both hands, then lunge with right hand and grab high rung for an instant.

Power-Building Exercises

When climbers use the term *power*, they are typically referring to the need to make a quick, strenuous reach or handhold grasp on steep terrain. This type of movement is the stuff of steep sport climbs and V-hard boulder problems.

Physiologically, your ability to move powerfully is a function of how fast muscular motor units can be called into play and how well they are trained to fire in unison. Effective power-training exercises must therefore target the nervous system with fast, dynamic motions that are far different from the strength- and endurance-training exercises covered in this chapter. Inherent to power training are high dynamic force loads, which provide beneficial training stimuli but also threaten the joints and tendons of the fingers, arms, and shoulders. For this reason, the following power-training exercises are inappropriate for beginning or recently injured climbers, as well as anyone lacking the maturity and discipline to follow the training and rest guidelines.

Adequate rest between power exercises and workout sessions is also crucial. As a rule, you should not engage in more than two power workouts per week. Furthermore, individual workouts should be relatively brief, as training intensity and speed is more important than training volume. In fact, performing a high volume of power exercises (or training power more than twice per week) is a prescription for injury. Constantly remind yourself that in training power, *less is more.*

Power Pull-Ups

This simple power-building exercise can be performed on any pull-up bar or fingerboard. Initially, you might train power exclusively by doing a few sets with this exercise—or you could just do a single set as "power warm-up" before executing one of the other exercises described below.

Will Mayo on Ginseng Route (5.12c)
Shagg Crag, Maine.
PHOTO BY ERIC McCALLISTER

1. Grip a pull-up bar or the largest holds on a fingerboard in the palms-away position. Your hands should be about shoulder width apart.

2. Now explode upward with the goal of completing the upward phase of the pull-up as fast as possible.

3. Pause at the top position for a moment, then lower yourself to the starting position at a slightly slower rate.

4. Upon reaching the bottom position, immediately explode upward with the next pull-up. Strive for as rapid a reversal in direction as possible—this rapid turnover is essential to optimal training.

5. Continue with these explosive pull-ups for a total of five to ten repetitions. Do not do more than ten reps, regardless of the feeling that you could continue on with the exercise.

6. Rest for three minutes before doing a second and third set.

Safety notes: Never drop forcefully onto straight arms; instead strive to change directions slightly before your arms reach full extension. Cease this exercise if you feel any pain in your elbows or shoulders.

Campus Training

Developed by the late, great Wolfgang Güllich at the Campus Center in Nuremberg, Germany, campus training is the current gold standard for developing upper-body power. This unique explosive exercise works the entire chain of climbing muscles, including the fingers and forearms, biceps, shoulders, back, and core, and hence for more than two decades it has been a staple exercise for countless top climbers. Unfortunately, campus training has also resulted in many finger injuries due to misuse or overtraining. As a guideline, this type of campus training is inappropriate if you are a climber of less than three years' experience; overweight; unable to climb at least 5.11 or boulder V5; have a recently injured finger, elbow, or shoulder; or lack the maturity to train properly and take adequate rest days. First, we'll look at Campus Laddering, followed by the more difficult Double Dyno exercise.

■ CAMPUS LADDERING

As the name implies, this exercise involves climbing in a hand-over-hand, ladderlike motion up the campus board with no aid from your feet. Unlike the campus training Double Dynos (described next), this laddering exercise uses controlled dynamic movements that are less likely to result in injury. Consequently, this is a better staple exercise for regular use, and you should only progress to the Double Dyno exercise upon gaining confidence in the capabilities and health of your fingers and arms.

1. Hang with nearly straight arms from the bottom rung of the campus board. Your hands should be about shoulder width or slightly less apart.

2. Striving for brisk, fluid motion, begin laddering hand-over-hand up the campus board using alternating rungs for your left and right hands. Your goal is to ascend the board as quickly as possible.

3. Match hands on the top rung, and then descend carefully by dropping hand-over-hand back down alternating rungs to the bottom position.

Campus Laddering:
Hang with both hands.

Ladder upward,
hand-over-hand.

4. Perform a total of six to twelve hand moves, never more. To increase difficulty, skip rungs as you hand-over-hand up the board.

5. Rest for three to five minutes before engaging in a second set.

6. Limit yourself to a total of three sets during your formative workouts. As you gain conditioning, you can do up to ten sets or begin a gradual shift to training with the Double Dynos.

Safety notes: Consider taping the base of your fingers to provide a little extra support to the finger tendons. Terminate your campus training at the first sign of pain in the joints or tendons of the fingers.

Training note: Laddering on small rungs tends to train contact (finger) strength more than upper-body power, whereas longer reaches on larger rungs better isolates one-arm power and lock-off strength.

Continue upward, hand-over-hand.

Match hands on top rung, then descend hand-over-hand.

Upper-Body Strength, Power, and Endurance Conditioning

■ CAMPUS DOUBLE DYNOS

This dynamic up-and-down, fully airborne exercise is widely recognized as true campus training. It's the most effective at producing neural disinhibition and building maximum contact strength and pulling power. This exercise is also the most stressful and potentially injurious exercise that climbers engage in, since the dynamic double-handed drops generate a force several times your body weight. Are your fingers and tendons ready for this level of stress? It's my belief that the answer is "no" for better than 95 percent of climbers. If you do think you are ready for this exercise—are you an elite climber with no recent finger, elbow, or shoulder injuries?—then introduce it gradually and cautiously.

1. Begin by hanging from a high rung on the campus board. (It's good to number your rungs beginning with the bottom rung as "number one.")

2. Simultaneously let go with both hands and drop to catch the next lower rung (number two).

Campus Double Dynos:
Hang with both hands from higher rung.

Drop, using both hands
to catch lower rung.

3. Immediately explode upward with both hands to catch the third or fourth (harder) rung. This is one full repetition, but don't stop!

4. Without hesitation, drop down to and again catch the second rung.

5. Explode back up to the third or fourth rung.

6. Continue this double-handed, drop-down-and-explode-up sequence between two rungs for up to six repetitions. Stop prematurely instead of risking a failed downward catch—and have a bouldering crash pad in place just in case.

7. Rest for three to five minutes before engaging in a second set.

8. Perform a total of just two or three sets during your formative workouts; however, you can build up to six sets (a combined total of Campus Laddering and Double Dynos) as you gain conditioning and confidence.

Immediately explode back upward with both hands.

Catch higher rung. Repeat without pause.

Campus Training Guidelines

- Engage in campus training only if you are an intermediate to advanced climber (able to climb least 5.11 or boulder V5) with at least three years' climbing experience and no recent history of finger or arm injuries. Double Dynos should be used only by highly conditioned, elite climbers.

- Warm up thoroughly. Spend at least an hour performing various warm-up activities and bouldering on increasingly more difficult problems before beginning your campus training.

- Reinforce your finger tendons with a few tight turns of athletic tape.

- Emphasize speed over volume. Completing three high-speed, explosive sets is far more beneficial than six sloppy, poorly executed sets with frequent pauses between hand moves.

- Do not campus train while in a state of high fatigue or if you have any doubts about the health of your fingers, arms, or shoulders.

- Immediately terminate your campus training session at the first sensation of pain in your joint or tendons.

9. Limit yourself to just one or two sessions per week, and cycle on and off campus training every two or three weeks.

Safety notes: Consider taping the base of your fingers (use the A2 method depicted on page 98). Terminate your campus training at the first sign of pain in your fingers, arms, or shoulders.

Training notes: Execute Double Dynos only on rungs that are 0.75-inch or more in depth. In terms of training stimulus, speed of repetitions is more important than the number of reps, distance traveled, or size of rungs. Specifically, strive to turn around the catch on the lower rung and lunge upward in a quarter second (hard, but ideal).

Rope and Ladder Climbing

Rope and ladder climbing is one of the very best ways to develop awesome upper-body power. Legendary boulderer John Gill used rope climbing as a staple training exercise, and years later John Bachar popularized inverted ladder training among climbers. Since the advent of indoor climbing walls, however, rope and ladder climbing has fallen largely out of use. Still, serious climbers in search of high-end power would be wise to incorporate some rope or

ladder climbing into their training programs. Both apparatuses provide for feet-off, campuslike movements, thus requiring a high level of base strength to execute. The equipment needs are either a 1.5-inch manila gym rope or a homemade Bachar Ladder.

1. After a lengthy warm up of pull-ups and upper-body stretching, begin from either a standing or a sit-down (harder) position.

2. Grip either the rope or a ladder rung with both arms at near full extension.

3. With an explosive two-arm pull, begin climbing up the rope or ladder in a fast, smooth, yet dynamic motion. The goal is to maintain steady upward motion for the duration of the ascent, although it will likely take you some time to develop this ability.

4. Upon reaching the top, slowly lower yourself arm-over-arm in a smooth, controlled motion. Dismount the rope or ladder—do not climb additional distance without a rest.

5. Rest for three to five minutes before making your next climb.

6. Perform three to five runs up the rope or ladder,

always taking an adequate rest so that you can make a high-quality effort.

Safety notes: On the descent, do not drop down in a fast, jerky manner that will shock-load your elbows and shoulders. Only use Bachar Ladders constructed with static rope. Stop rope or ladder training if you feel any pain in your elbows or shoulders.

Training notes: Highly conditioned individuals should strive to increase the speed of ascent instead of doing additional sets. As with all high-intensity exercises, it's best to cycle on and off this exercise every few weeks.

Anaerobic Endurance Conditioning Exercises

Detailed in this section are four of the most grueling exercises in this book. Training anaerobic endurance requires repeated, sustained bursts of exercise of a length and intensity that will elicit a significant release of lactic acid. These exercises are designed to do just that, and the result of each will be a wicked muscular pump and the hallmark burn of lactic acid. Of course, the payoff is that your body will respond to this stimulus in ways that will gradually improve your anaerobic endurance—and thus your ability to climb at a high intensity for an extended period.

Pull-Up Intervals

If you are tired of training pull-ups in the same boring way, Pull-Up Intervals offer a nice alternative that will definitely pump you up! Your goal is to complete twenty, one-minute Pull-Up intervals that comprise a set number of pull-ups and a rest period taking exactly one minute (aggregate). Use a stopwatch or clock with a second hand so that you can stay on an exact training schedule.

1. Start the stopwatch, mount the pull-up bar or fingerboard (use the bucket holds), and immediately commence doing five pull-ups. Strive for a smooth, steady pace that takes about two seconds for each complete repetition.

2. After doing five pull-ups, dismount and rest for the remainder of the one-minute interval.

3. At the one-minute mark, begin your next set of five pull-ups. Upon completion of the fifth pull-up, dismount and rest for the remainder of the second, one-minute pull-up interval.

4. Continue performing these five-repetition, one-minute intervals for a total of ten to twenty minutes. If you make it to ten minutes, you will have completed fifty pull-ups in aggregate—a pretty good intermediate-level pull-up workout. If you make it the full twenty minutes, congratulate yourself for doing one hundred pull-ups!

Training notes: If you cannot make it to at least the ten-minute mark, then reduce the number of pull-ups per set to just three or four. Conversely, increase the number of pull-ups per set to six or seven when you find the full twenty-minute, one-hundred-pull-up routine begins to feel less than grueling!

Rope and Ladder Climbing: Ascend with fast, powerful moves. Descend smoothly and steadily.

Frenchies: Pull up to top, hold, then lower to straight arms.

Pull up to top, lower halfway and hold.

Frenchies

Frenchies may be the best anaerobic endurance exercise for the pull muscles, but they are inherently painful due to the lactic acid released by the large muscles of your back and arms. The payoffs are significant and obvious, however, in terms of both more lock-off endurance on the rock and a marked increase in pull-up ability. Here are the details on this uniquely effective modified pull-up.

1. Mount a pull-up bar or fingerboard (use bucket holds) with your hands about shoulder width apart.

2. Pull up to the top position and lock off with your hands against your chest for a five-second count (*one thousand one, one thousand two*, and so on). Lower yourself to the bottom, straight-armed position.

3. Pull up to the top again, but this time lower yourself to the halfway position (elbow flexion of 90 degrees). Hold this position statically for a five-second count, then lower yourself to the bottom.

4. Pull up a third time, but this time lower yourself about two-thirds of the way (elbow flexion of

Pull up to top, then lower two-thirds of the way and hold.

120 degrees) to perform the static, five-second lock-off.

5. Lower to the bottom position and you will have completed one full cycle. But don't stop!

6. Without hanging to rest, immediately begin a second cycle of Frenchies. Repeat steps 2 through 5, being sure to hold all the lock-offs for a full five-second count.

7. Continue performing a third, fourth, and fifth cycle (very hard), if you're able. Stop when you can no longer perform a full pull-up or hold the lock-off.

8. Rest for five minutes before doing a second and third set.

Safety note: Despite the grueling nature of Frenchies, they are actually a very safe training exercise. Stop, however, should you develop any pain in your elbows or shoulders.

Steep-Wall Lock-Off

Of all the lock-off exercises, this is the most specific, since it is executed on a bouldering wall with actual climbing moves and body positions. It's also the best exercise for training the coveted lock-off endurance needed for long, steep routes.

This exercise is a good example of how you can creatively engage in targeted strength training on the typical home bouldering wall. The goal, of course, is not to actually climb a boulder problem but instead to isolate the lock-off muscles in a highly specific way that brings all the muscles of your arms, core, and legs into play. A wall over-hanging between 30 and 50 degrees past vertical is ideal. This is somewhat similar to the Campus Lock-Off exercise described earlier, except use of your feet reduces training resistance and makes it a longer-duration, bona fide endurance-training exercise.

1. Begin in a sit-down position below the wall so that you can grip two similar starting holds. A deep, positive hold or an incut HIT Strip or System Hold is best, since the goal of this exercise is to train lock-off endurance, not your grip.

2. Place your feet on any two holds on the "kick board" at the base of the wall and lift your rear end off the floor. This is your starting position.

3. Now, pull up on the handholds and lock off one arm, so that you can reach up with your other hand to touch—not grab onto—a hold at full arm reach. Allow your body to twist and tense as needed to make the lock-off solid.

4. Hold this lock-off position for two seconds before dropping back down to the starting position, with both hands engaging holds.

5. Immediately pull back up (both hands), lock off, and reach with your other hand to touch the highest hold possible. Hold this lock-off for two seconds, then return to the starting position.

6. Continue this lock-off-and-reach motion with alternating hands as long as possible without cheating on the two-second lock-offs or grabbing on with your reaching hand. Your training goal is a total of twenty to fifty lock-offs, which will result in between one and two minutes of exhaustive exercise.

7. Take a rest break, and then perform a second and third set. The length of rest you take will depend on your level of conditioning. For initial

Steep-Wall Lock-Offs: Place hands and feet in starting position.

Pull up, lock off right arm, and reach up with left arm to touch a distant hold.

training sessions, take a five-minute rest between sets. As your conditioning improves, reduce your rest to as little as one minute—an elite-level anaerobic endurance workout!

Safety notes: Like many climbing-specific exercises, Steep-Wall Lock-Offs are stressful on the elbows and shoulders. Engage in a complete warm-up before using this exercise, and conclude your session with some antagonist muscle training to strengthen the elbow and shoulder joints (see chapter 8).

Training note: Use larger hand- and footholds or a less overhanging wall if you cannot do at least twenty total lock-offs.

Lower back to starting position.

Pull up, now lock off left arm, and reach up with right arm to touch a distant hold.

Indoor walls provide an ideal platform for interval training, in which you alternate between climbing and resting.

PHOTO COURTESY OF NICROS, INC. CLIMBING WALLS, WWW.NICROS.COM

Climbing Intervals

This final exercise involves repeating laps on a moderately difficult boulder problem or climb. The ideal route would be steep and strenuous, yet not so technically difficult that you're unable to climb a few complete laps. The training protocol is to alternate climbing burns with rest intervals, much like the interval training performed by runners. The rest phase should be roughly proportional to the length of the climbing phase. Therefore, if your climbing phase involves sending a ten-move boulder problem (which might take about thirty seconds), you'd want to take a rest of only thirty seconds to, at most, one minute between burns. A longer climbing phase, such as lapping a steep sport climb or moving around your home wall for four minutes, should be followed by a similarly long rest.

1. Select a boulder problem or route that will be strenuous, yet at a level of difficulty that you can successfully ascend several times.

2. Climb the route, and then begin a rest period that's about equal to the length of time you were climbing. Resting any more than double the length of the climbing phase will diminish the training effect. Use a stopwatch so you stay within these guidelines.

3. After the rest period, begin your next interval. Climb the boulder problem or route, then take the prescribed rest break.

4. Continue with these climbing intervals until you can no longer complete the climb or boulder problem. If you can successfully perform more than five intervals, then select a slightly more strenuous climb for your next workout.

Safety note: Select routes that are void of tweaky holds or severe moves that might be injurious when climbed repeatedly and in an increasing state of fatigue.

Training notes: Recruit a training partner to climb during your rest breaks. The camaraderie and encouragement will help you hang on through the increasing pump and pain of this interval training. You can also engage in climbing intervals using the Tabata Protocol as explained on page 106.

Antagonist Muscle Conditioning

If you are serious about climbing your best and avoiding injury, then you must also be serious about training the antagonist muscles.

Climbers naturally obsess over strength training of the gripping, pulling, and lock-off muscles, since they are the agonist or prime movers in climbing. Conversely, the antagonist push muscles that oppose the pull muscles are often dismissed as "not important." This common misconception, and the resultant lack of push-muscle conditioning among climbers, is a leading cause of injury, particularly in the highly stressed elbow and shoulder joints.

The antagonist muscles used in climbing include the pectorals (chest), deltoids and trapezius (shoulders and upper back), triceps (back of the upper arm), and the finger extensors (outside of the forearm). Strength and flexibility in these muscles is fundamental to controlled, precise movement and for maintaining joint stability. Unfortunately, few climbers regularly engage in training of these antagonist muscles, while the agonist pull muscles get all the attention. Growing imbalance subsequently develops around the elbow and shoulder joints, thus increasing instability and risk of injury. Outside of the fingers, the most common injuries among

Thomas McConnell on **Rock Wars** *(5.10a), Red River Gorge, Kentucky.*
PHOTO BY DAN BRAYACK, WWW.BRAYACKMEDIA.COM

climbers are elbow tendinosis and shoulder subluxation and dislocation. You now know why.

Unlike acute finger tendon injuries, many elbow and shoulder maladies are avoidable given a modest investment in stretching and training of the antagonists, generally referred to as push-muscle training. As little as twenty minutes, two or three days per week, is all that it takes to maintain muscle balance and reduce injury risk. This chapter is divided into three sections that detail exercises for the forearms, the large push muscles of the chest and shoulders, and the small but vital muscles of the rotator cuff. I encourage you to include all these exercises in your weekly conditioning program. And as always, perform a general warm-up of light activity and stretching before engaging in this targeted strength training.

A final word of caution: Never train or stretch a freshly injured muscle, tendon, or joint. Pain in your fingers, elbows, or shoulders is a warning sign that something is wrong—cease climbing and training until you are pain-free. Also, it would be wise to see a doctor if you have any doubts about the cause of the pain you're experiencing or if you are unsure of the best course of treatment and rehabilitation for an existing injury. See page 197 for a list of useful reference books, including one on sports injuries.

Forearms

Relative to normal everyday use, no group of muscles works harder in climbing than the forearm muscles that produce finger flexion. As these workhorse muscles gradually grow stronger, a resultant imbalance with the underworked finger extensor muscles increases. The ultimate endgame for many climbers is elbow tendinosis.

Tendinosis on the outside of the elbow, known as tennis elbow, is ironically most common among climbers. It typically develops as a result of overtraining, climbing too often on crimpy routes, and disproportionately weak extensor muscles. Fortunately, you can likely avoid this injury by taking at least three rest days per week, regularly varying your climbing preference, warming up and stretching your forearm muscles before climbing, and disciplined training of Reverse Wrist Curls to maintain muscle balance.

Tendinitis on the bony inside of the elbow is less frequent, but it can also develop as a result of insufficient strength in the forearm pronator muscles or an acute trauma from an extreme move or one-arm pull. Once again, adequate rest along with regular stretching and supplemental training of the forearm muscles will reduce your injury risk. Let's take a look at the two most important exercises for maintaining elbow health.

Reverse Wrist Curls

This is mandatory exercise for all climbers to work the extensor muscles. Use this in conjunction with the forearm stretches provided in chapter 3 as part of your warm-up and cool-down ritual.

1. Sitting on a chair or bench, rest your forearm on the far end of your thigh so that your hand faces

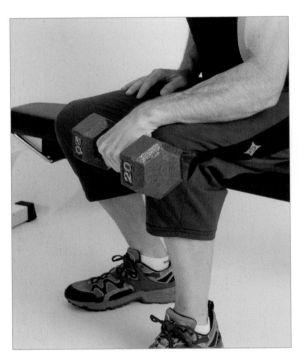

Reverse Wrist Curls: Hold dumbbell with palm facing down.

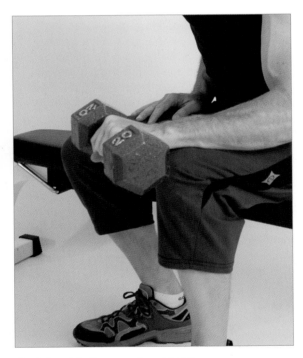

Curl dumbbell upward and hold.

palm-down and overhangs your knee by several inches.

2. Firmly grip a 5- to 15-pound (much harder) dumbbell, and begin with a neutral (straight) wrist position.

3. Curl the dumbbell upward until your hand is fully extended. Hold this top position for one second, then lower the dumbbell to the starting position.

4. Continue with slow, controlled reverse curls for fifteen to twenty repetitions.

5. Perform two sets with each hand, with a two- to three-minute rest between sets.

6. Use a heavier dumbbell if you can easily execute twenty repetitions. Well-conditioned individuals may need as much as a 25- or 30-pound dumbbell.

7. Alternatively, use a strong rubber band to similarly work the extensor muscles. Open your fingers against the band. Despite the seemingly small resistance, this simple exercise can provide a surprisingly good forearm-extensor workout.

Safety notes: Do some light forearm stretching before and after this exercise. Reduce exercise resistance if you feel any elbow or tendon pain while engaging in this exercise.

Alternate Extensors Exercise:
Use an exercise band.

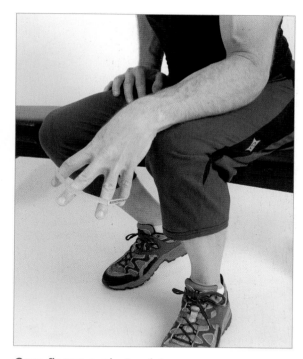

Open fingers against resistance
of the thick rubber band.

Pronators

Arm-pulling movements naturally result in supination of the hand. If you perform a pull-up on a free-hanging set of Pump Rocks, you'll discover that your hands naturally turn outward or supinate as your biceps contract. Consequently, training forearm pronation is an important antagonist exercise for climbers. There are several ways to train forearm pronation, but the easiest is with an ordinary sledgehammer.

1. Sit on a chair or bench with your forearm resting on your thigh, your hand in the palm-up position.

2. Firmly grip a sledgehammer with the heavy end extending to the side and the handle parallel to the floor.

3. Turn your hand inward (pronation) to lift the hammer to the vertical position. Stop here.

Pronators: Hold sledgehammer parallel to floor with hammer head out to side.

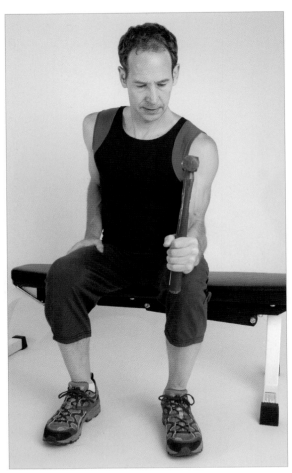

Turn hand inward, lifting hammer to vertical position.

4. Now slowly lower the hammer back to the starting position. Stop at the horizontal position for one second before beginning the next repetition.

5. Continue lifting the hammer in this way for fifteen to twenty repetitions. Choke up on the hammer if this feels overly difficult.

6. Perform two sets with each hand.

7. Alternatively, you can train pronation with an exercise band. Hold one end of the band in your hand with the excess hanging out the thumb side of your palm. Anchor the other end of the band around your leg or foot, and rotate your forearm while keeping it parallel to the floor.

Safety notes: Do some light forearm stretching before and after this exercise. Reduce exercise resistance if you feel any elbow or tendon pain.

Alternate Pronators Exercise:
Use an exercise band.

Anchor one end of band around foot.
Rotate forearm inward.

Upper Torso

Arm flexion and the hand-to-chest lock-off position are fundamental to almost every climbing movement. These pulling movements are powered by the large muscles of the arms and back—in fact, over time these toned and bulging pull muscles become the physical hallmark of the advanced climber. Unfortunately, beneficial gains in pull-muscle strength often lead to a functional imbalance with the opposing push muscles. Let's delve deeper into this important relationship.

The major push muscles of the upper torso and arms are the pectoralis muscles of the chest, the deltoids and upper trapezius of the shoulders and upper back, and the triceps of the back side of the upper arm. Each of these muscles plays an important role in climbing by stabilizing the shoulder joint

and in some cases directly contributing to locomotion (as in mantling). Maintaining a high level of conditioning in these push muscles is therefore vital for avoiding injury and supporting climbing performance.

In training the push muscles for climbing, the goal is to increase strength, endurance, and flexibility, but without an excessive addition of muscle mass. Consequently, the common weight-lifting strategy of working with the heaviest weight possible is the wrong push-muscle program for climbers! Instead you want to train with lighter weights (less than one-half your body weight) and higher repetitions. Following are four essential push-muscle exercises for the upper torso; later on you will learn two equally valuable exercises for training the smaller muscles of the rotator cuff.

Shoulder Press

The shoulder-press motion is the obverse of the pulling action of climbing—and thus no exercise is more central to antagonist muscle training. Although you can execute this exercise with a common health-club shoulder-press machine, performing dumbbell shoulder presses provides a more complete workout of the many small stabilizing muscles of the shoulders.

1. Sit on a bench with good upright posture and feet flat on the floor.

2. Begin with bent arms, palms facing forward, and the dumbbells positioned just outside your shoulders.

3. Press straight upward with your palms maintaining a forward-facing position. As your arms become straight, squeeze your hands slightly inward until the dumbbells touch end-to-end.

4. Lower the dumbbells to the starting position. The complete repetition should take about two seconds.

5. Continue this motion for twenty to twenty-five repetitions. Strive for smooth, consistent motion throughout the set.

6. Rest for three minutes and perform a second set.

Training notes: Women should start with five-pound dumbbells and advance to 10- or 15-pounders upon being able to do twenty-five reps. Most men can begin training with 15- or 20-pound dumbbells, then progress to 25 and 30 pounds as they are able to achieve twenty-five repetitions. In the long term it's best not to progress beyond 50 percent of your body weight (total weight lifted), since these heavier weights may build undesirable muscle bulk.

Shoulder Press: Begin with dumbbells just outside shoulders.

Press straight up; touch dumbbell ends.

Bench Press

The bench press is a staple exercise of power lifters and bodybuilders; however, it is also useful to a climber striving to maintain stable, healthy shoulders. The key for climbers is to use only moderate weight—begin with a total weight equal to about 25 percent of body weight and progress up to 50 percent (never more). For example, a 160-pound climber would begin training with two 20-pound dumbbells (40 pounds total) and progress up to training with, at most, 40-pound dumbbells or 80 pounds with an Olympic bar.

1. Lie flat on a bench with your legs bent and your feet flat.

2. Using an Olympic bar or two dumbbells, begin the exercise with your hands just above chest level and palms facing your feet. If you're using a bar, your hands should be a few inches wider than your shoulders.

3. Press straight up with a slow, steady motion. If you're using dumbbells, squeeze your hands together to touch the ends of the dumbbells together upon reaching the top position.

4. Return to the starting position, pause for a moment, and then begin the next repetition. If you're using a bar, be careful not to bounce it off your chest. The goal is slow, controlled movement that takes about two seconds per repetition.

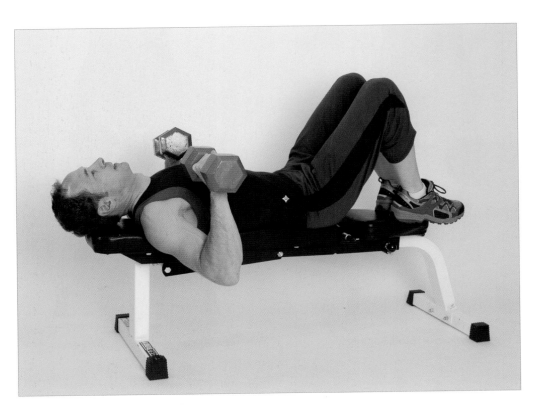

Bench Press: Begin with hands just above chest level.

5. Continue for twenty to twenty-five repetitions.

6. Rest for three minutes before performing a second set.

7. Alternatively, if weights are unavailable, you can use push-ups to provide a similar workout. Begin with your hands shoulder width apart and build up to doing two sets of twenty-five repetitions. When you accomplish this, start moving your hands closer together to increase training resistance. Beginners should do the push-ups with knees on the floor until they are able to progress to the normal feet-on-floor position.

Dips

Dips are an excellent exercise for strengthening the many muscles of the upper arm, shoulders, chest, and back. What's more, the dip motion is quite similar to the mantle move in climbing, and thus provides a very sport-specific benefit! Some health clubs and gyms possess a parallel-bar setup ideal for performing dips. Alternatively, you can use the incut 90-degree corner of a kitchen counter, or position two heavy chairs in a parallel position. Using a set of free-floating Pump Rocks or gymnastics rings is my personal favorite—they provide a more dynamic (and difficult) workout.

Press up. Touch dumbbell ends.

1. Position yourself between the rings, parallel bars, Pump Rocks, or other apparatus.

2. Jump up into the straight-armed starting position with your hands drawn in near your hips.

3. Slowly lower yourself until your arms are bent 90 degrees—do not lower beyond this point!

4. Immediately press back up to the starting position.

5. Continue this up-and-down motion, with each repetition taking about two seconds. Strive to complete ten to twenty (hard) repetitions.

6. Perform two or three sets with a three-minute rest in between each.

Safety notes: Don't rush or bounce through this exercise. Never lower yourself beyond a 90-degree arm bend. Stop immediately if you experience any shoulder pain.

Training note: Employ a spotter to help you complete ten repetitions if you cannot do them on your own. The spotter should stand behind you and lift around your waist or, more easily, pull up on your ankles (bend your legs to facilitate this).

Dips: Jump up into straight-armed position.

Lower into a 90-degree arm bend, then push back up.

Shrugs

This exercise strengthens the upper trapezius muscles, which run from the back of your neck across toward the top of your shoulders and back.

1. Stand erect with your arms by your sides and head facing forward. Hold equal dumbbells in each hand with your palms facing inward.

2. Now shrug shoulders upward as if trying to lift your shoulders to your ears. Do not bend your arms.

3. Pause at the top position for one second, then roll your shoulders backward slightly before lowering them back to the starting position.

4. Continue shrugging at a steady pace for twenty to twenty-five repetitions. Be sure to always pause for one second at the top of each shrug.

5. Rest for three minutes before performing a second set.

Safety notes: Bend at the knees when lifting the weights off the floor. Maintain a slight bend in your knees and good back and shoulder posture while engaging in this exercise.

Training note: Initially train with just a 5- or 10-pound dumbbell until you feel comfortable with proper execution. Gradually build up to using 15- to 35-pound dumbbells.

Shrugs: Stand erect with arms straight.

Shrug shoulders upward, pause, roll shoulders back slightly, and return to start.

Rotator Cuff

The shoulders are the most movable and unstable joints, and next to the fingers they are the most at-risk body parts for rock climbers. In particular, those of us with a preference for overhanging walls and V-hard boulder problems must recognize the potential for developing a shoulder injury that could plague us for years or even require surgical intervention. Every time we crank up a steep wall with an elbow pulled backward beyond the plane of our body, we are in jeopardy of subluxation. Furthermore, excessive hanging with straight arms produces an accumulated strain on the shoulders that can eventually lead to shoulder instability. The bottom line: Climbing—especially hard bouldering—is a minefield for the shoulders.

Knowing these dangers, a wise climber will be proactive in minimizing exposure to the most dangerous positions and engage in disciplined training of the stabilizing muscles that surround the shoulder. Use of the push-muscle exercises described above is paramount; however, there are several smaller muscles of the rotator cuff that should also be trained. Here are the two best exercises for isolating the small muscles used for internal and external rotation of the shoulder joint.

Internal Rotation

The many muscles that contribute to internal rotation of the shoulder are a common weakness among climbers. While the bench-press and shoulder-press exercises described earlier strengthen the larger muscles that contribute to internal rotation, this isolation exercise targets the smaller muscles that protect the front side of the rotator cuff.

1. Lie on your side with your bottom arm in front of your waist; place a rolled-up towel or a pillow under your head to support your neck. Rest your other arm along your hip and upper thigh.

2. Hold a 2- to 5-pound dumbbell in the hand of your bottom arm, positioning your forearm perpendicular to your body.

3. Lift the weight up to your body and hold for a moment before lowering it back to the floor. The upper portion of your arm should remain in contact with the floor throughout the range of motion—think of your upper arm and shoulder as a door hinge that allows your forearm to swing "open and closed."

4. Continue in a slow, but steady motion for a total of fifteen repetitions.

Internal Rotation: Hold dumbbell with forearm perpendicular to body.

5. Do two sets on each side, with a three-minute rest in between sets.

6. Alternatively, you can train internal rotation in the standing position using an exercise band. With your arm bent at 90 degrees and your elbow held by your side, pull the exercise band in toward your navel.

Safety note: Stop immediately if you experience any pain in your shoulder. Try using a lighter weight.

Training note: Increase weight in 1 or 2-pound increments, but do not exceed 10 pounds. Using heavy weight is not necessary and may even result in injury.

Alternate Exercise: Stand with arm bent at 90 degrees, and pull exercise band in toward navel.

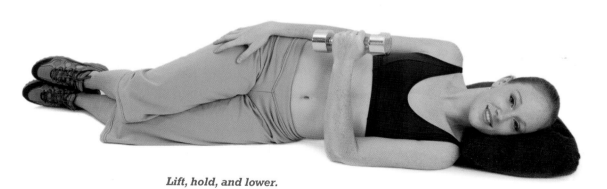

Lift, hold, and lower.

External Rotation

Many climbing movements result in external rotation, so these rotator cuff muscles are likely in better shape than those that contribute to internal rotation. Still, this exercise does isolate the smaller muscles in a unique and beneficial way.

1. Lie on your side with your bottom arm in front of your waist; place a rolled-up towel under your head to support your neck. Alternatively, you can bend your bottom arm and use it as a headrest.

2. Hold a 2- to 5-pound dumbbell in the hand of your top arm. Rest the upper arm and elbow on the top side of your body, and then bend at the elbow so that your forearm hangs down over your belly and the weight rests on the floor.

3. Now raise the weight upward toward the ceiling until your forearm passes a parallel position with the floor.

4. Pause at this top position for a moment, then lower the weight to the floor. Your upper arm should remain in contact with the side of your torso and act only as a hinge that allows your forearm to swing up and down.

5. Continue in a slow, but steady motion for a total of fifteen repetitions.

6. Do two sets on each side, with a three-minute rest between each set.

7. Alternatively, you can train external rotation in the standing position using an exercise band. With your arm bent at 90 degrees, your elbow held by your side, and your hand in near your navel, pull the exercise band outward.

Safety notes: Stop immediately if you experience any pain in your shoulder. Try using a lighter weight.

Training notes: Increase weight in 1 or 2-pound increments, but do not exceed 10 pounds. Use of heavy resistance is not necessary or desirable.

Alternate Exercise:
Stand with arm bent at
90 degrees and pull
exercise band outward.

External Rotation: Hold dumbbell in front of body.

Raise to parallel with floor, hold, and lower.

9

Stamina Conditioning

The benefits of stamina training include increased capacity to climb all day while maintaining a high level of performance throughout, resistance to fatigue when faced with an extraordinarily hard or sustained climb, faster recovery between climbs and days of climbing, and improved aerobic capacity.

Depending on your preferred type of climbing, the importance of stamina can range from minor to paramount. In bouldering, for example, the need for strength and power far exceeds that of stamina. Conversely, stamina supersedes strength and power for alpine and big-wall climbing. In the middle of this continuum are multipitch routes and all-day sport climbing, which require strength and power as well as significant stamina.

Think of stamina as your ability to resist fatigue while engaging in sustained or intermittent physical activity for an extended period of time. Some people refer to this attribute as endurance, since it is largely a function of aerobic and anaerobic endurance. Anaerobic endurance is the ability to sustain near-maximal exercise in which the local muscles produce

*The author on the East Buttress of **Middle Cathedral (5.10c), Yosemite, California.***

PHOTO BY KEITH McCALLISTER

energy in the absence of oxygen, whereas aerobic endurance is best viewed as the capacity for whole-body exercise of moderate intensity and extended duration, in which the energy is generated in the presence of oxygen. Chapters 6 and 7 provide numerous exercises for training anaerobic endurance local to the climbing muscles of the upper body. This chapter will focus primarily on training of aerobic endurance—what I will call stamina from here onward. However, you will notice some similarities to the anaerobic-endurance-training protocols detailed in chapter 7.

As in other types of conditioning, there are sport-specific and general methods of stamina training. The most specific—and therefore effective—approach is to train as you perform. In other words, to develop stamina for long days of cragging, you train by logging many long days at the crags. As a practical matter, this approach is not an option for many recreational climbers with daily commitments to job, school, family, and such. The best training alternative, then, is to engage in general stamina training, such as running and biking, coupled with a high volume of climbing whenever possible.

Long-term benefits of stamina training include increased capacity to climb all day while maintaining a high level of performance throughout, resistance to fatigue when faced with an extraordinarily hard or sustained climb, faster recovery between climbs and days of climbing, and improved aerobic capacity. These benefits are the result of numerous adaptations including increased VO_2 max (cardiorespiratory), increased capillary vascularity, increased central nervous system efficiency, and enhanced glycogen (muscle fuel reserve) storage.

Before we move on to the details of stamina conditioning, it's important to acknowledge a few nontraining influences on stamina. Quality of nutrition and level of hydration play a primary role in determining stamina (to be discussed in chapter 12). And perhaps overriding all physical factors, extraordinary stamina comes to those with uncommon willpower and tolerance to pain.

Stamina Conditioning for Bouldering, Sport Climbing, and Multipitch Routes

Excellence at bouldering and sport climbing requires abundant strength and power, precise technique and efficient movement, and a killer instinct, but very little in the way of stamina. The exception are long boulder problems and sport routes that do test anaerobic endurance (local to your forearm and upper-body pull muscles) and your body's ability to sustain exercise near or beyond its lactate threshold. While stamina training will have no real impact on your maximum-move ability, then, it will enhance recovery between climbs, as well as increase your anaerobic threshold and ability to persevere through long, sustained boulder problems or sport routes. Let's examine three different strategies for improving stamina for bouldering, sport climbing, and multipitch routes. Some of these strategies are similar to the muscular endurance exercises described in chapter 7, since stamina in a short-climb setting is largely a matter of anaerobic endurance.

Bouldering Circuits

Climbing through a timed bouldering circuit is the most specific form of stamina training for boulderers. The goal is to climb a series of moderately difficult problems with only brief rest intervals in between. Select problems that are a few grades below your maximum ability—a problem of the right grade should make you work, yet not test you maximally or cause you to fall off repeatedly. If you develop a deep muscular pump, it's important that you decrease the difficulty so you don't shift into training anaerobic endurance. With a home wall, you can set a series of problems and practice them over the course of a few sessions. At a commercial gym or if bouldering outdoors, you will need to suss out the right problems and determine an order that may decrease in difficulty slightly from beginning to end. Either way, it will take some planning and effort to develop an appropriate bouldering circuit for your ability.

For starters, I suggest you develop a circuit of ten problems; you can increase the length of the circuit to fifteen or twenty problems as your stamina improves. After a good warm-up, begin by sending the first boulder problem of the circuit. Take a two-minute rest, then fire off the second problem. Continue in this fashion through the complete ten- to twenty-problem circuit. Should you fall off a problem, shake out briefly and give it one more attempt. If you fall a second time on the same problem, begin your two-minute rest interval and then move on to the next problem. It's important to keep moving and stick to the prescribed schedule. Purchase a stopwatch (less than $10 at most sporting goods stores) to time precise two-minute rests between problems. This is a great thirty- to sixty-minute stamina workout!

Route Intervals

Route intervals are the sport climbers' analog to the bouldering circuit drill described above. The primary difference is that the climbing and rest intervals will be longer, thus making the drill highly specific to the physiology of climbing longer, roped routes. Although this drill can be performed at an outdoor crag, it's ideal for use at a commercial gym with many vertical to overhanging toprope and sport climbs.

The training goal is to climb five intervals, each comprising three to six minutes of climbing followed by three to six minutes of rest. The length of the rest period should be equal to the length of time spent climbing. Use a stopwatch to time both the climb and rest phases. You can execute this drill by changing routes for each interval or by using the same route for the full duration. I suggest you use a single route that you can wire and steadily ascend without a high risk of falling due to technical difficulties. These training intervals are best climbed at

Bouldering circuits are extremely practical and effective as stamina training for bouldering and sport climbing.

Interval training on a track is a highly structured and effective strategy for training anaerobic endurance and stamina.

PHOTO BY ERIC J. HÖRST

about 50 to 80 percent of maximum exertion, so you will likely need to select a route that is one and a half to three number grades below your limit. Stop climbing at a prescribed time (say, three minutes) instead of climbing to failure and falling off due to a deep muscular pump. Again, developing a deep pump is a sign you've shifted into training anaerobic endurance, which is not the goal with this routine. That said, by the end of your fifth interval you will feel worked and indeed have completed an awesome stamina-building workout.

Whether you are climbing route intervals or a bouldering circuit, ask your belayer or spotter to join in on the session. It's of great benefit to have a partner who's vested in the training—this will enhance motivation and create a training synergy that is mutually beneficial. Take turns timing each other with the stopwatch, and have fun!

Running Intervals

Competitive runners view interval training as the gold standard for increasing their capacity for moderate- to high-intensity running. These benefits come as a result of an increase in aerobic capacity (VO_2 max), anaerobic capacity, and lactate threshold. The long-term benefits of this training methodology are so profound that all serious medium- to long-distance runners incorporate some form of interval training into their monthly training cycles.

The physiological adaptations of running interval can also be a boon for serious rock climbers. While the act of running is hardly specific to climbing, its effects on the cardiovascular system are not far different from a long, multicrux route or the act of speed climbing. If you engage in any form of long, strenuous climbing, you can be sure that running intervals will improve your performance in terms of both improved stamina and enhanced recovery between efforts.

The most common interval-training program is to run alternating fast and slow laps on a track. Although you can also run intervals on a road or trail, the ease of setting a goal and gauging distances makes running on a standard 0.25-mile (400-meter)

Table 9.1 Sample Intermediate and Advanced Interval-Training Workouts		
	Intermediate (2 miles)	Advanced (3 miles)
Warm-up lap	1 lap slow	1 lap slow
Interval 1	½ lap fast	1 lap fast
	½ lap slow	1 lap slow
Interval 2	½ lap fast	1 lap fast
	½ lap slow	1 lap slow
Interval 3	1 lap fast	2 laps fast
	1 lap slow	1 lap slow
Interval 4	1 lap fast	2 laps fast
	1 lap slow	1 lap slow
Interval 5	½ lap fast	½ lap fast
	½ lap slow	½ lap slow

track preferable. For initial training sessions, set out to run 2 miles—that's an aggregate distance of fast and slow laps. As a rough gauge, your fast laps should feel like 80 to 90 percent of your maximum speed and be just fast enough that you cannot talk while running. Try to hold the fast pace for a complete lap, and then pull back to a jog for the slow lap. The slow-lap pace should be modest enough to allow you to catch you breath and chat with a training partner. Continue alternating fast and slow laps (or half laps) for a total of eight.

Unlike many forms of training for climbing, regular interval training will provide a measure of training gains. Use a stopwatch to time the length of your interval-training sessions and you will have a definitive metric for gains in conditioning. Over the course of several weeks and months, your decreasing 2-mile workout times will confirm that your aerobic capacity and lactate threshold are increasing. As your level of conditioning improves, consider increasing the length of your workout to 3 miles. To further increase training stimulus, you could progress to running two fast laps followed by just one slow lap. Be creative, mix it up, and have fun with this off-the-wall training for climbing!

Stamina Conditioning for All- and Multiday Climbing

If your climbing goals include sending Grade IV or V routes in a day, climbing big walls, or venturing onto alpine terrain, then stamina conditioning is quite possibly the most important type of fitness training. Clearly, the best way to train for all-day climbing stamina is to frequently climb all day. Most recreational climbers, however, have neither the time nor the opportunity to do enough climbing to train stamina in only this way. Fortunately, the more general forms of aerobic training will build stamina that carries over to these pursuits. In this section I'll detail three different strategies for building abundant stamina.

Climb All Day

This is the train-as-you-climb strategy. If your climbing goal is to send Grade IV or V routes in a day,

then you need to simulate this workload as often as possible. In preparing for a trip to Yosemite, for example, you could train at your local crag by logging ten, fifteen, or twenty pitches in a long day. Reaching these training goals will take repeated efforts to extend what you are capable of performing not only physically, but also technically and mentally. Climbing a large number of pitches in a day requires both efficient movement and an efficient two-person climbing system. Stamina gains are really an aggregate of enhancements in your ability to perform mentally and physically to a higher level of precision and total volume.

It's important to begin this type of stamina training at least three months before the date of your target climb. Plan your training and climbing schedule so that you can engage in climb-all-day stamina training at least once every two weeks and ideally once or twice per week. Clearly, no amount of running or other type of physical stamina conditioning can duplicate or replace this most specific and valuable training method. So get a partner and start climbing!

Two-a-Day Workouts

Two-a-day training is a powerful training strategy of endurance athletes. The goal here is to engage in two, one- to two-hour workouts per day. This could include any combination of aerobic activities, such as running, biking, or swimming and a climbing session comprising bouldering, gym climbing, or half a day at the crags. To maximize the quality of each workout, it's important to have at least a six-hour break between the two. For example, you might go for a long run in the morning, and then climb for a couple of hours in the evening, or vice versa. If climbing is not an option, you would simply perform a morning and late-day aerobic activity of an hour or more each time.

This is, of course, is a lot of training and requires a high level of conditioning that might take a few months to build up to. Furthermore, you should begin with just one two-a-day workout per week and gradually advance to as many as three two-a-day routines per week. Maintaining proper

Mountain biking and trail running are
two popular methods of stamina training.

hydration and eating between the two daily workouts is vital—eating to enhance recovery in preparation for your next workout is central to effective stamina training and performance.

Ultradistance Conditioning

Ultradistance conditioning—whether it be climbing, biking, or running—is all about pushing beyond what you are accustomed to in terms of total volume and rigor. This step-by-step one-upmanship of yourself results in a "callusing effect." The benefit of this mind–body callusing is that upon defining a new limit—running your first marathon, climbing your first big wall in a day, or whatever—repeating this feat in the future will not seem as difficult as the first time. In doing it the first time, you develop a "callus" that enables you to perform to this same level more easily in the future.

How much of this adaptation is mental and physical is hard to say, but it's an effect that every ultradistance athlete knows well. You, too, can experience and leverage this callusing effect by engaging in stamina workouts and days of climbing that exceed your previous limit. You might do this by adding a 0.5-mile to your long-distance run each week or by climbing one more pitch or 100 feet more vertical distance during a day at the crags. The best marathon runners and ultraclimbers typically dedicate one day per week to performing a super-volume of physical activity that approaches or exceeds their performance goal or previous limit. Make this your target, too.

As your workout volume increases, it's fundamental that your volume of rest between workouts also increase. Extreme stamina training coupled with too little rest will quickly lead to illness or injury. A high-volume training day may require three or more days of rest before you are ready for a repeat workout. In ultra-stamina-performance situations, such as climbing several grueling back-to-back days on a big wall or a high-elevation ascent, the deep level of fatigue that develops often requires one to four weeks for complete recovery.

PART IV

Climbing-
Specific
Conditioning

Conditioning Programs

Injury Prevention

General
Conditioning

Conditioning Principles
and Self-Assessment

Performance Nutrition

10

Design Your Own Conditioning Program

Excellence in climbing requires a commitment to work on all facets of the game—improving technique, refining mental skills, and increasing your level of physical conditioning.

The first nine chapters have provided the many puzzle pieces that make up an effective conditioning program. In this chapter you will learn how to piece together the dozens of exercises and training strategies to create an optimally effective conditioning program.

Central to designing the best program for *you* are the results of the self-assessment from chapter 2. Review the graph of your assessment profile on page 22 to see how you scored in each of the eight areas that influence climbing performance. The lowest scoring areas represent the most immediate constraints to further gains in ability. While some of these areas relate to experience, lifestyle, and mental attributes, several are a direct reflection of your current level of physical conditioning and body composition. This chapter will guide you in design-

ing a program that effectively addresses the critical areas of general and sport-specific conditioning, skill development, injury prevention, and nutrition. Just how you approach each of these areas and which one or two you will most strongly focus on is a matter of your general ability level—beginner, intermediate, or advanced—and the results of your self-assessment. Focusing your efforts on improving the lowest-scoring areas is essential for obtaining optimal results.

As your training feeds back positive results, it's imperative that you modify the focus and makeup of the program to accurately address emerging new constraints. Remember that the limiting constraints on your performance are a moving target—to hit the bull's-eye, you must regularly correct your aim. Retake the self-assessment every few months and use the results to redirect your program. Failing to do this—and executing the exact same climbing workouts—is tantamount to chaining yourself to a set ability level.

Let's take a look at the guidelines for an effective beginner, intermediate, and advanced conditioning program. Consult table 10.1 to determine which program is most appropriate for you.

The talented and well-trained Emily Harrington pulling down at the Sendfest competition.

PHOTO BY ERIC J. HÖRST

Table 10.1 Classifications of Ability

Review the bullet points below, and circle all that apply.
Classify yourself in the group with the most circles.

Beginner	Intermediate	Advanced
• < 1 year climbing	• Actively climbing > 1 year	• Actively climbing > 3 years
• Toprope ability < 5.9	• Toprope > 5.9	• Onsight lead ability at 5.11 trad and/or 5.12 sport
• Little or no lead climbing experience	• Lead climbing up to 5.10 trad or 5.11 sport	• Boulder >V6
• Poor physical conditioning and/or overweight	• Boulder V2 to V6	• Aggregate self-assessment score >165
• Aggregate self-assessment score < 120	• Aggregate self-assessment score 121–165	

Beginner Climber's Program

The first step to becoming a better climber—and getting into climbing shape—is simply to climb on a regular basis. Therefore, the most important part of a beginner's conditioning program is to climb three or four days per week. No other training activity will increase your climbing fitness as fast as actually going climbing. That being said, there are several good reasons to engage in supplemental training. First, a modest amount of aerobic training can benefit your climbing by improving stamina and body composition. Similarly, some basic strength and flexibility training will facilitate learning of climbing moves on increasingly strenuous terrain. Finally, some basic push-muscle conditioning will help mitigate the muscular imbalances—and injury risk—that commonly develop as climbing-specific strength increases.

As you progress into the realm of being an intermediate climber—say, breaking into 5.10 and 5.11 climbs—you will need to progress to a more targeted program of climbing-specific exercises.

However, the hallmark of a well-designed beginner-level program is precisely that it's *not* highly specific. Many enthusiastic novice climbers make the mistake of advancing to the highly stressful, sport-specific exercises too soon. Not only does this tempt injury, but it also handicaps your learning of skills and, ultimately, rate of improvement. Follow the program below and you'll safely progress to an intermediate level in a year, perhaps sooner.

Warm-Up and Stretching

Every workout or climbing session should begin with a period of warm-up and stretching activities. Spend ten to twenty minutes performing a selection of warm-up activities and stretches from chapter 3. Conclude your warm-up by climbing a few easy, large-hold boulder problems or moderate toprope routes.

Climbing Skills Training

As emphasized above, time spent actually climbing is the best training investment—it will yield improvements in your technical and mental skills as well as physical fitness. Warming up and executing general conditioning exercises are important, but time spent on the wall should make up the majority of your workout. For example, a two-hour climbing-gym workout might begin and end with fifteen minutes of stretching and general training, respectively, while ninety minutes of climbing constitutes the core of the session. Similarly, a day of outdoor climbing should begin with a period of warm-up and stretching before you ever step onto the rock. Often the hike in to the cliff will provide an excellent warm-up, so that you only need to execute five to ten minutes of stretching before beginning to climb. If you climb half a day or less, consider doing a thirty-minute session of general conditioning exercises upon completion of your climbing.

Making the most of your climbing time requires climbing with intention—an intention to refine your climbing skills, challenge yourself on new terrain, and develop the vital mental skills of problem solving, visualization, self-awareness, and thought control. The areas of technique and mental training are gold mines rich in potential for rapid improvement. Here are a few improvement strategies to leverage.

When climbing outdoors, it's important to climb at many different areas so as to expose yourself to a wide range of technical and tactical demands. Each new climbing area visited will build unique skills and therefore grow your technical and cognitive abilities. Another excellent learning strategy is to follow a more accomplished climber up a near-limit (for you) multipitch route—this experience will stretch your mental and physical boundaries and help redefine what you view as possible. Alternatively, you can toprope a difficult single-pitch route a few times with the goal of perfecting your movements and ascent as if it were a gymnastics routine. Incorporating all of these strategies into your outdoor-climbing experience will put you on the fast track to the next level of ability.

Inherent to indoor climbing are both limitations and advantages in terms of training skill. The character of artificial walls obviously limits the potential to learn climbing skills, since no indoor wall can mimic what Mother Nature offers in terms of breadth and depth of technical demands and rigor. Fortunately, indoor walls do provide an ideal setting for learning and refining many fundamental skills. A regular schedule of indoor climbing will produce rapid learning of motor skills while also developing a moderate level of physical strength. You can accelerate this process further by incorporating specific technique- and mental-training drills into your session. Detailing the many different climbing drills is beyond the scope of this book, but you'll find dozens of powerful practice drills in my books *Learning to Climb Indoors* and *Training for Climbing.*

General Conditioning

An effective beginner-level conditioning program must also include a modest amount of general fitness training. Depending on the results of your self-assessment in chapter 2, you may need to invest as little as fifteen minutes twice per week, or as much as forty-five to sixty minutes four days per week, on general conditioning exercises. The most important consideration is your current body composition—excessive body fat or bulky muscles in the wrong places will have a strong negative impact on your climbing performance. In this case regular aerobic exercise is of as much importance as is climbing a few days per week. Perform your aerobic activity at the end of your climbing workout or on nonclimbing days. Revisit chapter 4 for exercise and diet tips for optimizing your body composition.

General strength training is also worthwhile as long as it doesn't divert your time and focus away from actual climbing. Ideally, you would engage in fifteen to thirty minutes of general conditioning exercises at the end of your climbing session. Performing the six body-weight exercises described in chapter 4 along with a few of the antagonist muscle exercises in chapter 8 is all that's really needed. The antagonist training can be performed on your climbing or nonclimbing days; however, the pull-muscle and core exercises should be used only on regular climbing days (or in place of climbing days if it's not possible to get to a gym or crag).

Designing Your Program

Designing an effective beginner-level conditioning program is not as complex as you might expect. First, consider that the global goals of this program are pretty straightforward: developing climbing skills, improving general fitness, and avoiding injury. More specifically, you must shape the program such that it addresses the weaknesses identified in your self-assessment. Leverage the appropriate chapters and exercises that best target your limiting constraints. Piecing together a specific routine that you will have time and energy to regularly complete is key. Here are some guidelines for creating a daily conditioning program and weekly training schedule.

First, you must always distinguish between climbing and nonclimbing workouts. Given the availability of a climbing wall, crag, or boulders, your goal should be to engage in up to four climb-

ing workouts per week. All other conditioning activities—aerobic training, antagonist conditioning, and such—must be fit into your weekly schedule while still allowing at least one or two days of complete rest per week. Table 10.2 depicts two sample microcycles to use as templates in scheduling your weekly conditioning activities.

Once you've penciled in a schedule of workout and climbing days, it's time to plan the body of each workout. While exceedingly long workouts are not necessary (or advisable), you should plan on spending between one and three hours on a typical workout. For example, a nonclimbing workout of aerobic training and general conditioning exercises might take a little over an hour to complete, whereas a gym-climbing session followed by some general conditioning exercises will take two to three hours. Either way, your workout should be structured to

Table 10.2 Sample Microcycles for Beginners

Four-Day-per-Week Climbing Schedule

Monday	Tuesday	Wednesday	Thursday	Friday	Saturday	Sunday
Rest day or aerobic training	Climb and general conditioning (see chapters 3, 4, and 5)	Rest day or aerobic training	Climb and general conditioning	Rest day	All-day climbing	Climb or general conditioning and aerobic training

Weekend-Only Climbing Schedule

Monday	Tuesday	Wednesday	Thursday	Friday	Saturday	Sunday
Rest day or aerobic training	Aerobic training and general conditioning (see chapters 3, 4, and 5)	Rest day or aerobic training	Aerobic training and general conditioning	Rest day	All-day climbing	All-day climbing

Table 10.3 Beginners' Climbing- and Nonclimbing-Day Workout Templates

Climbing Day	Nonclimbing Day (in place of a climbing day)
• Warm-up and stretching (10–20 minutes).	• Warm-up and stretching (10–20 minutes).
• Indoor or outdoor climbing (60–90 minutes or more if climbing outdoors). Note: Emphasize learning over performance.	• General conditioning (30–60 minutes). Note: Train pull and core exercises, followed by antagonist exercises, per chapters 4 and 5.
• General conditioning (15–30 minutes). Note: Train pull and core exercises, followed by antagonist exercises, per chapters 4 and 5.	• Aerobic Conditioning (20–40 minutes).
	• Cool-down stretching (5–10 minutes).
• Cool-down stretching (5–10 minutes).	

begin with some warm-up and stretching activities, then progress to climbing activities (if any are planned), and then conclude with general conditioning exercises and any aerobic training. Table 10.3 outlines two sample workout plans. Consult chapters 3, 4, and 5 to select specific stretches, activities, and exercises to plug into each section of the workout.

Intermediate Climber's Program

Given the steep improvement curve during the formative stage of learning, it's common to reach the intermediate level in a year or two, if not sooner. A hallmark of the intermediate, however, is a much slower rate of improvement that may even seem imperceptible as you near the advanced ability level. This apparent plateau in performance (which often coincides with breaking into the 5.10 or 5.11 grade), on the heels of a year or more of steady gains, can be extremely frustrating. But instead of reacting negatively to such a leveling-off in performance gains, recognize that it is a normal stage of the progression—and one you will rise above given a quality effort. With this realization, you are empowered to begin a new training program that

will trigger a new growth phase and soon-to-be-success at the lofty grades of 5.11 and 5.12!

Embarking on a new training program must commence with an acute understanding of your true strengths and weaknesses. Take the self-assessment in chapter 2 to obtain fresh insight of the specific areas you need to improve upon and thus target with training. This initiative also demands that you embrace some new training strategies like hypergravity and interval training, as well as increasing your total commitment to climbing. Furthermore, you must make a conscious, sustained effort to elevate your climbing techniques, tactics, and mental game. Vow to seek out unfamiliar terrain and the types of climbs you have been avoiding up to this point, and then work these routes without ego or a need for success. Willfully exposing yourself to such climbs—and opening yourself up to the possibility of frustration and failure—not only builds character but is in fact the only pathway to becoming a climber of uncommon ability.

One trap to avoid as you progress toward becoming an advanced climber is that of mimicking the training program of other climbers. Doing this goes against the principle of individuality explained

The 4-3-2-1 Training Cycle

The 4-3-2-1 Cycle is a ten-week program comprising four weeks of technique and stamina training, three weeks of maximum strength and power training, and two weeks of anaerobic endurance conditioning. The cycle ends with a week of active or passive rest. Let's take a closer look at each phase of this cycle.

Phase 1: Four Weeks of Skill Training and Stamina Conditioning

The first four weeks of the training cycle are all about climbing for volume to develop technique and stamina. During this phase you should strive to climb outside as much as possible, with the goal of ticking as many routes as possible of different style and character. Distance climbed and experience gained should be your training benchmark, not absolute difficulty achieved. Ideally, you will log four days per week of combined indoor and outdoor climbing. You can also utilize some of the stamina-training routines described in chapter 9, especially if you are unable to climb four days per week.

Sample exercises Submaximal climbing for volume on an indoor wall, long days at the crags (no projecting), and various aerobic-training activities.

Phase 2: Three Weeks of Maximum Strength and Power Training

This second phase of the cycle is all about developing upper-body strength and power, and thus requires a completely different MO from phase one. The benchmark for gauging the effectiveness of your workouts is training intensity, not volume. Bouldering and hypergravity training are the ideal training activities, since both require short, intense efforts. Supplemental training should be limited to the strength and power exercises detailed in chapters 6 and 7.

Sample exercises: Hard bouldering, HIT, campus training, Weighted Pull-Ups, hypergravity bouldering, Uneven-Grip Pull-Ups, Weighted Fingerboard Hangs, rope climbing, and One-Arm Lunging.

in chapter 1—you possess unique strengths and weaknesses, experience, genetics, and goals, so your optimal program will be unlike that of any other climber. Strive to increase self-awareness and to proactively self-direct your training program in a way that is optimal for you. You may also benefit from the objective analysis and input of a climbing coach. Inquire at your local gym to see if they have a trained coach on staff, or visit www.usaclimbing.org for a list of coaches by region.

Let's examine the components of an effective intermediate-level conditioning program.

Warm-Up and Stretching

A period of warm-up and stretching is an important precursor to a successful workout or day of climbing. Although this ten- to twenty-minute warm-up may seem so simple that it's expendable, it is in fact essential for individuals of advancing ability, who frequently expose muscles and tendons to a level of stress not before experienced. The bottom line: A brief warm-up primes the muscles and joints for peak performance and injury prevention. Make it a habit.

Climbing as Training

Time spent climbing must always be the central element of your training program, since moving over stone is the only effective pathway to increasing your climbing skills and mental abilities. Many intermediate climbers come to form a climbing pref-

Phase 3: Two Weeks of Anaerobic Endurance Training

Linking many hard moves together takes anaerobic endurance, and phase three of the cycle is all about improving this capability. During this two-week phase, your focus narrows to climbing short, steep sport routes or long (twenty-plus-move) boulder problems of near-maximum difficulty. Exercise intensity should be mainly in the 80 to 90 percent of maximum range, but not so hard that you reach muscular failure in less than twenty total hand moves or one minute of climbing. In fact, the goal of anaerobic endurance training is to exercise at an intensity that never quite pushes you to failure. The anaerobic endurance exercises and climbing intervals described in chapters 6 and 7 are ideal. It's important to note that anaerobic endurance training places a large amount of stress on the neuromuscular system, and the accumulated stress of long-term use can lead to the overtraining syndrome. Consequently, it's best to limit yourself to between six and eight anaerobic endurance workouts over this two-week phase. Ironically, many climbers unknowingly train this way for months on end and then wonder why they hit a performance plateau or end up injured.

Sample exercises Route/HIT/Bouldering Intervals, Frenchies, Pull-Up Intervals, Steep-Wall Lock-Offs, and Fingerboard Moving Hangs.

Phase 4: One Week of Rest

The ten-week cycle concludes with a full week off from serious training. Although one to three days of rest between individual workouts is typically enough, executing a strenuous training cycle produces accumulated wear and tear on the joints and tendons, central fatigue of the nervous system, and mental fatigue that requires a more extended break. This week of rest will clear the slate of central fatigue and give your connective tissues time to catch up in the healing and recovery. During this seven-day break, you can engage in some active rest activities such as hiking and jogging; however, you should do no climbing movements or exercises. Dismiss worries that you might lose some conditioning during this rest period—in reality, you will be at your strongest at the end of the rest week.

Sample exercises, if any: Light "active rest" exercises such as stretching, Pilates, and easy running, biking, or hiking.

erence such as bouldering, indoor climbing, sport climbing, or crack climbing. While specializing will foster rapid gains in one of these subdisciplines, long-term improvement requires that you continue to gain experience and add skills in a wide range of climbing and rock types. There's a synergistic feedback effect that benefits those who strive for all-around proficiency as rock climbers.

An excellent practice strategy is to vary the type of climbing you engage in every few days or weeks. Regularly alternating among bouldering, steep sport climbing, crack climbing, vertical face climbing, and even slab climbing is like taking skill-building steroids. Not only will you develop an uncommonly broad skill set, but you'll also train your muscles and nervous system in a variety of valuable ways. This leverages the principle of periodization, which rewards those who regularly vary the focus, intensity, and length of their workouts.

While you might simply ad-lib your periodization by switching your climbing focus every week or so, it's best to plan out a more structured schedule. I advocate use of a cyclic workout program that varies climbing and training focus over the course of ten weeks. Such a program is more interesting and motivating, and it will provide superior results compared with training in the same ways week after week. Learn how to leverage the power of a training cycle by reading about the 4-3-2-1 Training Cycle in the box above.

Supplemental Pull-Muscle, Finger, and Core Conditioning

It is undeniable that harder, steeper climbs with smaller holds and longer moves demand a higher level of finger and lock-off strength, pulling and lunging power, muscular endurance, and core conditioning. Therefore, in addition to time spent climbing, an intermediate climber must begin some targeted training of the sport-specific muscles of the upper body and core. Chapters 5, 6, and 7 provide more than thirty different exercises for developing climbing-specific strength, power, and endurance.

Once again, the principle of periodization underscores the importance of varying your training focus every few weeks. In using the 4-3-2-1 Cycle described above, you would select exercises that build stamina for four weeks, maximum strength and power for three weeks, and then muscular endurance for two weeks. Selecting the appropriate type of climbing and exercises for use in each phase of the 4-3-2-1 Cycle is the key to maximizing the training effect and providing uncommonly good results!

If you climb three or four days per week, it's important that you perform these supplemental exercises at the end of your climbing session and not on rest days. Depending on the volume and intensity of your climbing, you might execute anywhere from three to six different supplemental exercises. It would be wise to skip the supplemental exercises at the end of a severe day of climbing that leaves you sore or exhausted.

If you are limited to climbing just once or twice per week, however, it's essential that you engage in thirty to sixty minutes of supplemental strength training once or twice per week. For example, you might execute eight or ten different exercises from chapters 5, 6, and 7 on Tuesday and Thursday, and then go climbing on Saturday and Sunday.

Antagonist Muscle Conditioning

If you are serious about climbing your best, then you must also be serious about training the antagonist muscles. A modest investment of fifteen minutes, three days per week, is all it takes to adequately train these muscles, thus improving joint stability and reducing risk of common elbow and shoulder injuries. Perform one to two sets of each exercise in chapter 8, either at the end of your climbing session or on rest days between climbing.

Designing Your Program

Designing an effective training program must begin with a long-term vision of your goals for the year ahead. These goals may be specific climbs to ascend, a grade to achieve by the end of the season, or just to be in top condition for weekend climbing or a big road trip. Mark target achievement dates on a calendar, along with the dates of possible weekend climbing trips, competitions, or other major events.

Given this framework you can now decide whether you want to begin a 4-3-2-1 Training Cycle or proceed with a self-directed train-as-you-go program. Most climbers get better results given the structure of the 4-3-2-1 cycle, even if it has to be occasionally broken for a few days due to conflicts or a brief road trip. If you choose the self-directed program, it's important that you still plan out your workouts at least a week in advance. Only this way will you be sure to schedule enough rest days as well as intelligently premeditate a workout plan for optimal results. Unfortunately, self-directed programs that lack proper planning eventually morph into random or redundant workouts of minimal effectiveness. The key to excellent results is not training harder, but training *smarter*—and planning your workouts in advance and acting in accordance with the principles of effective training is the essence of smart training.

Regardless of whether you use the 4-3-2-1 Cycle or a self-directed program, you should use a microcycle to integrate the various types of training into your weekly schedule. Table 10.4 offers several training microcycles that will help you integrate your climbing time, pull-muscle training, antagonist training, and aerobic training into a weekly schedule. The four-day-per-week climbing schedule is optimal; however, if there are no indoor walls or crags near your locale, you can still train to great benefit using one of the weekend-climbing only microcycles.

Table 10.4 Sample Microcycles for Intermediates

Four-Day-per-Week Climbing Schedule 1

Monday	Tuesday	Wednesday	Thursday	Friday	Saturday	Sunday
Rest day or aerobic training	Climb and pull-muscle and antagonist training (see chapters 5, 6, 7, and 8)	Rest day or aerobic training	Climb and pull-muscle and antagonist training (see chapters 5, 6, 7, and 8)	Rest day	All-day climbing	All-day climbing, aerobic training, or pull-muscle and antagonist training

Four-Day-per-Week Climbing Schedule 2

Monday	Tuesday	Wednesday	Thursday	Friday	Saturday	Sunday
Rest day or aerobic training	Climb and pull-muscle and antagonist training (see chapters 5, 6, 7, and 8)	Climb and pull-muscle training	Aerobic and antagonist training	Rest day	All-day climbing	All-day climbing or general conditioning and aerobic training

Weekend-Only Climbing Schedule 1

Monday	Tuesday	Wednesday	Thursday	Friday	Saturday	Sunday
Rest day or aerobic training	Pull-muscle and antagonist training (see chapters 5, 6, 7, and 8)	Rest day or aerobic training	Pull-muscle and antagonist training (see chapters 5, 6, 7, and 8)	Rest day	All-day climbing	All-day climbing or general conditioning and aerobic training

Weekend-Only Climbing Schedule 2

Monday	Tuesday	Wednesday	Thursday	Friday	Saturday	Sunday
Rest day or aerobic training	Pull-muscle and antagonist training (see chapters 5, 6, 7, and 8)	Pull-muscle training	Antagonist and aerobic training	Rest day	All-day climbing	All-day climbing or general conditioning and aerobic training

Table 10.5 Intermediates' Climbing and In-Place-of-Climbing Workout Templates

Climbing Day Workout	In-Place-of-Climbing Workout
• Warm-up and stretching (10–20 minutes).	• Warm-up and stretching (10–20 minutes).
• Indoor or outdoor climbing (60–90 minutes, or more if climbing outdoors). Note: Select type of climbing according to current phase of 4-3-2-1 Cycle.	• Sport-specific and core exercises (40–60 minutes). Note: Select exercises according to current phase of 4-3-2-1 Cycle.
• Sport-specific and core exercises (15–30 minutes). Note: Select exercises according to phase of 4-3-2-1 Cycle.	• Antagonist exercises (10–15 minutes).
• Antagonist exercises (10–15 minutes).	• Aerobic conditioning, if any (15–30 minutes).
• Cool-down stretching (5–10 minutes).	• Cool-down stretching (5–10 minutes).

As for the particulars of your climbing workouts, consult table 10.5 for an outline of how to best structure your climbing and in-place-of-climbing workouts. Per the microcycles shown in table 10.4 your goal is to engage in a total of four climbing-specific workouts per week. Out of the remaining three days per week, schedule one or two rest days and one or two days of supplemental aerobic training or antagonist training.

Finally, there's the matter of structuring a training schedule over an entire season or the calendar year. Although such macroscale planning can be difficult, there's great benefit to roughing in a tentative schedule of climbing trips, training cycles, and time off from climbing. First, long-term planning is essential for producing the greatest strength gains and climbing improvements of the course of a season. Furthermore, a training macrocycle enables you to plan out training in order to produce a peaking effect for an important road trip or competition. Finally, mapping out your climbing and training up to a year in advance empowers you to schedule some time away from climbing each year without adversely affecting your level of conditioning for important events. I strongly advocate a monthlong break from climbing every twelve months to facilitate a recharging of your motivation and the healing of any of those nagging physical pangs that commonly develop over a season of climbing. Some folks enjoy taking this month off around the Christmas holidays, whereas climbers in southern cities often prefer taking their break during the peak of the summer heat. Table 10.6 shows how one climber filled in her macrocycle over the course of a season. Make copies of the blank macrocycle in appendix B to use in your annual planning.

Advanced Conditioning Programs

If you on-sight 5.12, boulder V7 and above, or frequently climb big walls or alpine routes, then in the context of this book you are an advanced climber in need of an advanced training program. While the

Table 10.6 Training and Climbing Macrocycle

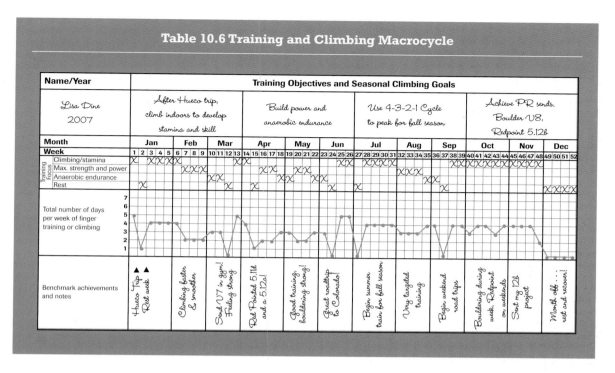

potential for further refinement in the areas of technique and the mind must never be overlooked, taking your game to the next level will definitely require greater physical prowess. The physical abilities you need to elevate are highly specific to your area of specialization. This is a critical distinction—to perform at the highest levels as a boulderer, sport climber, or big-wall or alpine climber demands an extremely specific training program that targets the particular limiting constraints of that type of climbing.

Figure 10.1 depicts the limiting physical constraints across the continuum of climbing subdisciplines. Bouldering, multipitch routes, and alpine climbing each places unique demands on the muscles, the cardiovascular system, and the energy systems used to fuel muscle action. Bouldering requires

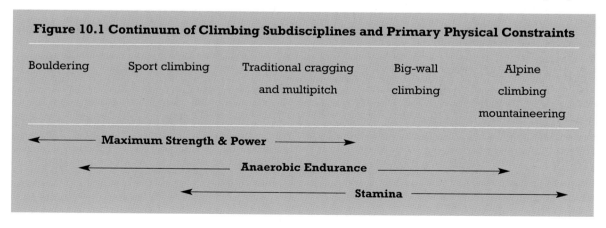

Figure 10.1 Continuum of Climbing Subdisciplines and Primary Physical Constraints

brief powerful movements and maximum strength, for example, whereas climbing a multipitch route demands muscular endurance and stamina with only occasional calls for power. Meanwhile, most big-wall and alpine routes require high levels of muscular endurance as well as vast stamina, but much less in the way of raw power and limit strength. The bottom line: Advanced climbers must target their training on the specific physical traits and energy system predominantly used in their preferred type of climbing, in addition to the global constraints identified by the self-assessment.

Another important—and often overlooked—element of an advanced conditioning program is supplemental training of the antagonist muscles. Many high-level climbers come to suffer elbow, shoulder, and even lower-back injuries due to muscular imbalances resulting from years of climbing-specific training. Extraordinary levels of strength in the finger flexor muscles of the forearms, the pull muscles of the upper arms and back, and the core muscles of the torso can lead to joint instability due to comparatively low levels of strength in the muscles antagonist to these prime movers. Fortunately, regular training of these opposing muscles will improve balance and stability and therefore reduce injury risk. Fifteen to thirty minutes of training, two or three days per week, is all you need to reap the benefits of antagonist conditioning.

Now let's examine the key elements for designing an effective conditioning program for bouldering and sport climbing, multipitch cragging, and big-wall and alpine climbing. Unlike the beginner- and intermediate-level programs described earlier, the strategy here is to narrow the scope of your training and focus primarily on the physical limitations of your current endeavors. In outlining a basic program for each of these three categories, it's assumed that you already possess ideal body composition, exceedingly high technical and mental skill levels, and above-average awareness of personal strengths and weaknesses. While the self-assessment in chapter 2 may uncover an unknown Achilles' heel, advanced climbers typically understand their true limiting constraints and thus recognize what they

need to train (or give up) in order to reach the next level of performance.

Conditioning for Bouldering and Sport Climbing

As illustrated in figure 10.1, bouldering and sport climbing place a premium on maximum strength and power as well as anaerobic endurance. The muscles of interest are obviously those used to grip the rock, pull up and lock off, and maintain body tension on steep terrain. Consequently, the exercises described in chapters 5, 6, and 7 must make up the main course of your training "feast."

As in all conditioning programs described in this book, the workout should begin with a warm-up period and then progress to climbing, climbing exercises, antagonist exercises, and aerobic activity (if any), concluding with a cool-down of light stretching. In designing the climbing and climbing exercise portion of the workout, it's best to train either maximum strength and power or anaerobic endurance on any given day (see table 10.7 for sample workouts). Training both in a single workout is not ideal; in fact, you will obtain the best training results by concentrating on a single facet—either anaerobic endurance or maximum strength and power—for a week or two at a time. Two possible approaches would be to alternate your training focus every week (that is, a week training maximum strength and power followed by a week of anaerobic-endurance training) or to follow a 3-2-1 Cycle of training maximum strength and power for three weeks, followed by two weeks of anaerobic-endurance training, and then up to one week of rest.

Allowing adequate rest between workouts is essential for reaping the full benefits of your training and for avoiding overtraining. Use one of the weekly microcycles in table 10.4 as a template for creating a weekly schedule with adequate rest days. Three nonclimbing days per week is your minimum allotment—take additional days off if you feel like you are training tired or getting weaker (a sign of under-resting).

An occasional four- to seven-day break from training and climbing is another good investment

Table 10.7 Sample Advanced Workouts for Bouldering and Sport Climbing

Maximum Strength and Power Workout	Anaerobic-Endurance Workout
• Warm-up and stretching (10–20 minutes). Note: Select exercises and stretches from chapter from 3.	• Warm-up and stretching (10–20 minutes). Note: Select exercises and stretches from chapter 3.
• Maximal bouldering or sport climbing (30–60 minutes, or more if climbing outdoors). Note: Select short, severe problems/routes that you will send (or fail on) in anywhere from 10 seconds to at most one minute.	• Work longer boulder problems and sport climbs (60–90 minutes, or more if climbing outdoors). Note: Select problems or routes that require sustained efforts of 2 minutes or longer.
• Maximum strength and power training exercises (30–60 minutes, or less if training after outdoor climbing). Note: Select several strength/power exercises from chapters 6 and 7.	• Anaerobic endurance exercises (30–60 minutes, or less if training after outdoor climbing). Note: Select several anaerobic-endurance exercises from chapters 6 and 7.
• Antagonist and core exercises (10–30 minutes). Note: Select several exercises from chapters 5 and 8. Antagonist exercises could instead be performed on rest days from climbing.	• Antagonist and core exercises (10–30 minutes). Note: Select several exercises from chapters 5 and 8. Antagonist exercises could instead be performed on rest days from climbing.
• Cool-down stretching (5–10 minutes).	• Cool-down stretching (5–10 minutes).

for hard-training climbers. Taking such a break every month or two will not only help you avoid the black hole of overtraining, but also create a peaking effect—that is, after this four- to seven-day rest, you will be the strongest for attempting a personal best route or major project. Similarly, it's advantageous to utilize a training macrocycle to integrate your conditioning program and rest breaks with dates of climbing trips or competitions. Make copies of the blank macrocycle in appendix B, and use it to keep track of your weekly training and schedule a long-term program for optimal results.

Conditioning for Cragging and Multipitch Climbing

Traditional cragging and multipitch climbing fall in the middle of the climbing continuum (figure 10.1), and therefore demand all-around conditioning with a significant reserve of strength and power, anaerobic endurance, and stamina. The conditioning strategy here is not unlike that described for the intermediate-level climber on page 161. The primary difference is that advanced climbers have higher tolerances for both training and climbing—with more years of experience and a higher level of conditioning, these experts must train and climb with higher intensity and greater volume to experience further gains in conditioning.

The 4-3-2-1 Cycle described earlier is an excellent framework by which to periodize training for optimal results. While such a ten-week schedule may be difficult to abide by during peak climbing season, it would be wise to implement it during an off-season period or between major trips. When possible, however, you want to vary the focus of your climbing every few workouts (or weeks) so as to work each of the three physical demands shown in the climbing continuum.

Planning your weekly workout schedule should be done at least a week in advance, so that you can schedule three or four days of climbing and at least three rest days. Supplemental targeted training for upper-body strength, power, and anaerobic endurance should always be performed on your climbing days, not on the rest days from climbing. Exposing yourself to more than four days of sport-specific activity per week is a prescription for overtraining and negative results.

The details for individual workouts will depend heavily on whether you are climbing outdoors, working indoors, or just strength training on a given day. Ideally, you want to do some form of climbing on each of your three or four workout days per week—a home climbing wall is an invaluable resource if access to a commercial gym or local crag is impractical on weekdays. As shown in table 10.8, your workouts should begin with a warm-up period, followed by an extended session of climbing. Pick problems and routes that will target the physical demand of the day—maximum strength and power, anaerobic endurance, or stamina.

After an hour or two of climbing, transition into your targeted training exercises for the day. Consult chapters 5, 6, and 7 to select a few exercises that match the training theme of the day. For example, if anaerobic endurance is your training focus du jour, you'd want to execute a few of the finger and upper-body exercises that work anaerobic endurance, such as Fingerboard Pyramids or Moving Hangs, Light Finger Rolls, Pull-Up Intervals, and Frenchies. Use the rest breaks between sets to perform a couple of the core-conditioning exercises, such as Hanging Knee Lifts, Aquaman, and the Bridge.

As stressed throughout this book, two days of antagonist training is mandatory for all climbers. Depending on the length of your workout and energy reserves, you could close out your workout with a few antagonist muscle exercises, or you could perform them on a rest day from climbing. Either way, consider two sets of dips, push-ups, shoulder presses, and Reverse Wrist Curls the

Table 10.8 Sample Workout for a Multipitch Climber

- Warm-up and stretching (10–20 minutes).

- Indoor or outdoor climbing (60–120 minutes, or more if climbing outdoors), with focus on either maximum strength/power, anaerobic endurance, or stamina. Note: Select type of climbing according to current phase of 4-3-2-1 Cycle.

- Sport-specific and core exercises, or aerobic-training activity (30–60 minutes). Focus on training maximum strength/power or anaerobic endurance during the three- and two-week phases, respectively. Engage in mainly aerobic training during the four-week stamina phase. Note: Perform few, if any, supplemental exercises after a full day of climbing.

- Antagonist exercises (10–20 minutes).

- Cool-down stretching (5–10 minutes).

absolute minimal requirement. See chapter 8 for details of these and other antagonist exercises.

A final training element that's often overlooked by multipitch climbers is stamina training. If you frequently put in long fifteen- to twenty-pitch days, then you likely possess a high level of stamina. Without a doubt, high-volume climbing is the most specific way to train stamina. For many weekend warriors, however, a significant portion of stamina training will have to be done off the rock. Chapter 9 provides several options, including running intervals and two-a-day aerobic exercises. Once again, you can best integrate stamina workouts into your program through use of the 4-3-2-1 Training Cycle. You would engage in a four-week phase of stamina training before moving on to three weeks of strength and power training. The cycle concludes with two weeks of anaerobic endurance and a week of rest. Then you start anew with four more weeks of stamina training.

Conditioning for Big-Wall and Alpine Climbing

The physical demands of big-wall and alpine climbing are as different from those of bouldering as running a marathon differs from the 100-meter dash. As shown in figure 10.1, muscular (anaerobic) endurance and stamina are the primary physical constraints for big-wall and mountain climbing, whereas power and maximum strength are essential for bouldering. Therefore, an effective conditioning program for big-wall and alpine climbers will be vastly different from the programs described on the preceding pages.

As an advanced climber, you likely have a few big-wall or alpine ascents already under your belt. Ask yourself the question: *What were the constraints on these previous climbs that prevented me from climbing faster, harder, and longer?* As in all forms of climbing, such limitations are commonly a complex blend of mental, technical/tactical, and physical issues. Constantly remind yourself that taking your game to the next level requires acute attention to improving in all of these areas. Since the focus of this book is the physical domain, let's examine how you can get into better shape for future ascents and expeditions.

First, you need to consider what aspect of your physical conditioning is most likely to inhibit you on upcoming climbs. If your goal is climbing a big wall in a day, then muscular endurance would be your primary constraint (being able to pump through many strenuous pitches in short order), with stamina a definite secondary limitation (having the full-body stamina and energy reserves to keep moving for twelve to eighteen hours). Given the goal of mountain climbing, however, these physical constraints are likely reversed. Hiking and climbing for several days at elevation is largely a matter of stamina, although there will certainly be sections of climbing (or even steep hiking) that will test your muscular endurance.

Designing a most effective program for reaching your goals, therefore, requires that you train as you will climb. If you are a big-wall climber, however, you obviously can't train on big walls every day; nor could an alpine climber live and climb in the mountains year-round. Still, you can train in a way that mimics the physical demands of these endeavors. Here's how.

■ CONDITIONING FOR BIG WALLS

If big-wall climbing is your passion, you would do best by improving muscular endurance. Training two to four days per week with a variety of endurance-conditioning exercises from chapters 6 and 7 would hit the mark. Of course, the exercise of sending many hard pitches in a half or full day is the ultimate method of training muscular endurance, so you should never pass up an opportunity to go climbing (up to four days per week) in place of exercise training.

In terms of stamina conditioning, nothing surpasses the benefit of frequent dawn-to-dusk days of climbing. You may only be able to log a few of these marathon-climbing days per month, however, so use the training alternative: two-a-day workouts as described in chapter 9.

The most effective two-a-day strategy is to combine a long run in the morning with a couple of hours of afternoon or evening climbing. Alternatively, you could engage in two aerobic workouts or

Table 10.9 Two Microcycles for Big-Wall Climbers

Two-a-Day Workout Microcycle 1

Monday	Tuesday	Wednesday	Thursday	Friday	Saturday	Sunday
Rest day with brief antagonist training	A.M. run and P.M. climbing with anaerobic endurance focus	A.M. run and P.M. climbing with anaerobic endurance focus	Rest day with brief antagonist training	Rest day	All-day climbing	All-day climbing, or twice-a-day running

Two-a-Day Workout Microcycle 2

Monday	Tuesday	Wednesday	Thursday	Friday	Saturday	Sunday
Rest day with brief antagonist training	A.M. run and P.M. run or bike	Rest day with brief antagonist training	A.M. run and P.M. run or bike	Rest day	All-day climbing	All-day climbing

two climbing workouts in the same day. Regardless, both the morning and evening workouts must be of sufficient duration to tap your reservoir of stamina. Going bouldering for thirty minutes or jogging a couple of miles won't do it. As a guideline, consider forty-five minutes for aerobic exercise and one hour of actual climbing time to be the minimum investment. Twice this amount would be ideal for a highly conditioned climber training for elite-level ascents.

Table 10.9 provides two microcycles for integrating weekday training and weekend climbing. Given the high demands of your program, quality rest and nutrition (see chapter 12) play a significant role in determining your rate of recovery and absolute gains in physical conditioning. Regular antagonist muscle training is another indispensable part of your program, as are warm-up and stretching activities. Remember, excelling as an advanced climber requires an excellent conditioning program and the discipline to not overlook or skip any detail, no matter how subtle or seemingly unimportant.

On a much larger scale, the magnitude of your year-to-year gains in conditioning and success on the rock will be a function of how well you plan your seasonal training as well as your ability to remain uninjured. Incur a finger, elbow, or shoulder injury and you may lose a few months of climbing and experience a setback in your overall level of conditioning. The planned rest days each week and the occasional planned week off from serious training and climbing are invaluable for keeping your mind and body in good working order. Use the blank macrocycle in appendix B to schedule your training and rest days around climbing trips, recovery periods, and other important life events.

■ CONDITIONING FOR ALPINE ASCENTS

Outside of the immense technical and logistical demands, success on alpine climbs often comes down to physical and mental stamina. Whether the goal is a one-day, base-camp-to-base-camp ascent of an alpine wall or a multiday summit push up a major peak, you can never possess too much stamina and confidence in your physical capabilities. Like an ultramarathoner running a 50- or 100-mile race, knowing that you've done it before *and* that you are in condition to do it again is a powerful realization that will carry you through to completion. Consequently, possessing a high level of conditioning as you set off on your expedition is as important as possessing the right equipment and climbing partners.

Although all-around fitness is a necessity, excelling on long climbs at elevation comes down to the master skill of economic movement combined with a massive reservoir of stamina. Frequent practice at the types of climbing you will be faced with in the mountains—crack, face, mixed, and such—is critical for developing the movement and tactical skills needed for fast, efficient climbing. Physically, your capacity to perform at a high level will be a function of total stamina and your ability to persevere through brief periods of hard climbing that require muscular endurance. While the big-wall climbing program described above is certainly

useful for the alpine climber, you also have a great need to grow stamina with some ultradistance conditioning. Follow the ultradistance-conditioning guidelines provided in chapter 9.

In the case of a major climb or expedition upcoming in a few months, you could begin with six weeks of the big-wall program (above) followed by six weeks of targeted ultradistance conditioning. Taper back the training volume at least three weeks before the trip, and do no strenuous training for the final seven to fourteen days before you are to begin the actual ascent. Use the training macrocycle in appendix B to plan your training between major climbs and trips. For example, schedule a three- to four-month pre-expedition training program ending with a one- to two-week period of rest leading up to your first climbing day. Then after the expedition, schedule a rest period of a length equal to the duration of your expedition. While this may seem like an excessively long break from training, it's a demonstrable fact that high-altitude and ultramarathon expeditions take a tremendous toll on the body that requires weeks, not days, to recover from.

Special Training Considerations

The beauty of climbing is that anyone can experience the wonder of the sport. Simply by moving over stone, you tap into a life force that transcends ability, gender, and age. That's the power of climbing!

While climbing used to be an activity dominated by twenty- and thirty-something men, it is now popular among women, teenagers, and even the over-fifty crowd as well. The beauty of climbing is that anyone can experience the wonder of the sport—in fact, each of the above-mentioned special groups possess unique mental and technical gifts that can be leveraged for extraordinary success! Still, women, younger climbers, and "senior" participants do have some special considerations to account for, mostly relating to strength training and potential for injury. If you are a member of one of these demographic groups, this chapter will touch on a few key issues that you should be aware of in planning and executing an effective conditioning program.

Conditioning for Females

The unique physiological traits of female climbers result in both assets and liabilities when it comes to climbing performance. On the plus side, females

*Sabrina Hague leading the mega-classic **High Exposure (5.6), Shawangunks, New York.***

PHOTO BY MATT CALARDO

possess shorter fingers, a lower center of gravity, and better flexibility than males, which enhances grip of small finger holds, more favorably positions weight over the feet, and facilitates a greater range of footholds and body positions, respectively. In terms of liabilities, females possess a higher average percent body fat and less natural upper-body strength than their male counterparts.

Fortunately, these physical limitations can be largely erased via an effective conditioning program. The serious female climber must then embrace the general and sport-specific strength training exercises described in chapters 4 through 8. In fact, such strength training is imperative for female climbers looking for high-level performance, since lack of muscular strength and local endurance is a common limiting constraint. Specifically, training should focus on increasing maximum strength in the upper-body pulling muscles, the antagonist push muscles, and the core muscles of the torso. In the formative stage of conditioning, it's vital to leverage less-than-body-weight exercises such as Aided Pull-Ups and Bench Dips described in chapter 4. As strength-to-weight ratio increases, there's no reason why the female climber can't "train like a man" with all the advanced techniques such as interval training, hypergravity training, and such.

Female climbers would also be wise to engage in some aerobic conditioning as a means of reducing percent body fat. In most cases, positive adaptations will result from a modest investment of twenty to forty minutes of running, three or four days per week. Of course, improved dietary surveillance combined with regular aerobic activity will bring

Conditioning Tips for Female Climbers

- Fall in love with strength conditioning! Training the pull muscles, antagonists, and core three days per week will have a profound effect on your climbing.

- Engage in regular aerobic activity. In particular, running for twenty to forty minutes a few days per week will favorably change your body composition and improve stamina.

- Go bouldering. Even if roped climbing is your preference, spending a few hours per week bouldering will help develop strength and power.

- Work routes just like men do. Frequently working on a climb at your limit—via toprope or hangdogging on lead—is a great physical workout, as well as a powerful way to develop technical and mental skills.

Cameron Hörst, age 6, toproping Ace in the Hole *(5.10a), Tuolumne, California.*

about the fastest changes in body composition. For more information on this, see the section on weight-loss strategies in chapter 4.

Conditioning for Juniors

It's undeniable that junior athletes learn complex sports skills more rapidly than adults, and in recent years we've seen many wunderkinder take the climbing world by storm with their V10 and 5.13 ascents, in some cases before the age of thirteen! These featherweight prepubescent climbers can hang on to small holds with little effort and can pull through steep terrain with high efficiency. Still, it's crucial to recognize that these young climbers naturally lack the maturity, self-awareness, and life experience to transfer their sport-climbing prowess to a wide range of climbing pursuits. They are also not physically prepared for the full rigors of serious sport-specific training as outlined in this text.

The best training for preteens is simply to climb three or four days per week. Additionally, they can safely engage in some basic conditioning such as body-weight exercises (pull-ups, push-ups, dips,

Abdominal Crunches, and such) and basic dumbbell exercises to train major muscle groups for more strength and balance. Disregard any old wives' tales you've heard that "strength training is not for kids." The American Academy of Pediatrics and the American College of Sports Medicine both support basic strength training for kids.

A junior climber entering puberty can gradually begin use of the sport-specific exercises detailed in chapters 6 and 7, but the most stressful—such as campus training and HIT—should not be used until near the end of puberty (age sixteen or seventeen). Throughout the preteen and early teenage years, it's vital that the primary training focus remain on improving climbing efficiency through mastery of the mental and technical skills. Given this approach, many junior climbers will advance to extraordinary levels without an excessive commitment to strength training.

The most common setbacks for teenage

Tips for Junior Climbers

- Focus on climbing, not training. Climb up to four days per week with an emphasis on skill development and having fun!

- Favor general conditioning with body-weight exercises. Youth climbers (under age thirteen) should train primarily with pull-ups, push-ups, dips, and core-conditioning exercises. Well-conditioned teenage climbers can add more advanced conditioning exercises. Targeted climbing-specific exercises as described in chapters 6 and 7 can be used up to three days per week.

- Engage in regular training of the antagonist muscles. The rapid strength gains that come with puberty can result in significant muscular imbalances and perhaps even injury. Training the antagonist muscles two or three days per week will greatly reduce injury risk.

- Strive for high-quality nutrition and abundant sleep. Teenage athletes should not engage in dieting and must have eight to ten hours sleep per night.

Tips for Over-Fifty Climbers

- Always warm up before training and climbing. Engage in at least twenty to thirty minutes of warm-up activity and stretching exercises.

- Avoid wildly dynamic exercises and climbing moves. Strive to climb statically and with great prudence when encountering severe body positions and moves.

- Engage in a comprehensive training program. Commit to a wide range of training, including aerobic activity, general conditioning, climbing-specific training, and antagonist conditioning.

- Leverage your wisdom and skill to prevail on hard routes despite physical limitations. Make improving climbing technique and mental skills a lifelong endeavor, and you will be a climber for life!

climbers are overuse injuries in the tendons, joints, and bones of the fingers, including stress fractures and damage to the growth plates. Juniors experiencing chronic pain in the fingers (or elsewhere) should cease climbing for a few weeks and consult a doctor if the pain continues. As a hard-and-fast rule, climbing and training for climbing must be limited to an aggregate of four days per week. The guidance of an adult climber or coach is extremely beneficial both in helping structure workouts and in monitoring rest and nutritional habits.

Conditioning for Over-Fifty Climbers

As adult climbers age, numerous physiological changes combine to form an increasing constraint on performance, especially beyond the age of fifty. A few of the unfortunate changes include reduced VO_2 max (aerobic capacity), decreased muscle mass, lower proportion of fast-twitch muscle fibers, and slower recovery. Despite these inevitable life changes, you can still climb at a very high level given a renewed focus on the mental and technical aspects of climbing and a steady dose of strength training. I know of more than a few fifty- and sixty-somethings who climb 5.12, ascend big walls, and trek in the mountains. You can, too, given a three-pronged approach of injury avoidance, physical conditioning, and mastery of skills.

Injury Avoidance

Unlike the resilient teenage body, older climbers are susceptible to injury during every single workout and climb. Common injuries range from muscle pulls to dislocated shoulders, torn tendons, and a variety of other joint and spinal problems. Fortunately, you can significantly reduce your risk by engaging in a comprehensive warm-up before every training and climbing session. While a younger climber might rush through a warm-up with just a few minutes of stretching, older climbers would be

Sixty-nine-year-old Charles Ganote
sending The Decameron (5.10b),
New River Gorge, West Virginia.
PHOTO BY ERIC McCALLISTER

wise to complete a full thirty-minute warm-up of general aerobic activity, light exercise, stretching, and easy climbing. Such a progressive warm-up will markedly decrease injury risk by warming and lengthening the muscles and spreading synovial fluid to lubricate the joints. While thirty minutes of nonclimbing exercise might not be your idea of a good time, it will enhance the quality of your climbing and reduce the risk of a muscle or joint injury that might lay you up for months or even knock you out of climbing completely.

Another way the mature, disciplined climber can avoid injuries is simply by avoiding potentially injurious moves while climbing. The goal is to foster a level of kinesthetic awareness where you can assess—or often intuit—the risk potential of a given move. Whether it is an awkward-feeling drop-knee, a tweaky-feeling pocket, or an improbable-feeling lunge, your discipline to heed the sensory feedback and rapidly evaluate the situation before forging onward can save you. Ultimately, you will need to make a quick decision as to whether you should retreat from the risky-feeling move, test the move once to see how if feels, or just push onward with the belief that you will succeed without incident. As a rule, the older you get, the more you should view such a risky-feeling move as a stop sign instead of a caution sign.

Physical Conditioning

Physical conditioning for over-fifty climbers is not all that different from the program I prescribe for the mass of climbers. You can safely employ most of the exercises contained in this book. Most of your limitations relate to dynamic, forceful training exercises, which become increasingly dangerous with advancing age. Climbers over fifty years of age would be wise to not engage in the most dynamic forms of campus training, One-Arm Lock-Offs or One-Arm Pull-Ups, frequent lunging, and steep V-hard bouldering. Of course, every climber possesses different generic encoding, experience, and physical capabilities, so there are surely a few senior climbers who prevail through the most stressful endeavors. But for the vast majority of older climbers, dynamic training is dangerous training.

Otherwise, your fitness-training goals are similar to those of every other climber: Optimize body composition, improve aerobic capacity and stamina, and increase muscular strength and endurance. Use the self-assessment test in chapter 2 to provide a focus to your training, then follow either the beginner-, intermediate-, or advanced-level workouts outlined in chapter 10.

Preplanning workout and rest days is of great importance for the older climber. Too many back-to-back workout (or climbing) days, too little rest, and poor nutrition over just a few consecutive days will crack open the door to possible injury or illness. Compound this over several weeks and it will open the door wide. Once injured and sick, the reduced immune efficiency and changing hormone levels of an older climber mean slower recovery and a faster drop-off of physical conditioning than for a younger climber. The bottom line for over-fifty climbers: Train, rest, and eat on a calculated schedule that will reduce injury risk, and do nothing to tempt injury.

Technical and Mental Mastery

The best older climbers are usually Zen masters who leverage the fact that climbing performance is two-thirds technical and mental and only one-third physical. By exploiting superior skill and wisdom, and bringing many years of experience to the table, older climbers can become true masters of rock by climbing very near their maximum capability. Whether that top capacity is 5.8 or 5.13, you can spot these elder masters by their measured approach, smooth sailing through scary terrain, and even the occasional calculated lunge or grunt that shows they are still willing to pull out all the stops to send.

Developing such mastery takes many years; in fact, in a complex sport such as climbing you can still acquire and refine mental and technical skills even after ten or twenty years' experience. So while your physical capabilities may be steady or waning, you can often compensate for this by improving mentally and technically. While describing skill practice methods and mental strategies is beyond the scope of this book (see *Training for Climbing*), it's important to point out that the only pathway to improvement in these areas is to actually go climbing! Consequently, you should strive to strike a balance between fitness training—still an important part of the equation—and going climbing at one of the myriad wonderful crags around the world. And, after all, isn't that the bottom line? Simply by moving over stone, you tap into the life force that climbing provides, which transcends ability, gender, and age. That's the power of climbing!

Nutrition, Workout Recovery, and Injury Prevention

Nonworkout time is just as important as time spent at the gym. Sports nutrition, rest and recovery, and injury prevention complete your conditioning program.

The final facet of an effective conditioning-for-climbing program relates to workout recovery and injury prevention. While the act of working out provides the stimulus for elevating physical performance, neuromuscular adaptations and growth occur primarily during nonworkout recovery periods. Therefore, becoming the best-conditioned climber you can be requires a conscious effort to eat and rest in ways that optimize recovery and lower injury risk.

Unfortunately, many climbers give little thought to these nonworkout aspects of effective conditioning—after all, it's what you do in the gym and on the crags that really matters, right? Of course, this couldn't be further from the truth, as nutrition and rest habits are the obverse side of the conditioning-for-climbers coin. Not only will poor rest and nutritional habits slow recovery and limit strength gains, but chronic under-resting and malnutrition will eventually suck you into the overtraining syndrome with its telltale decline in overall strength and performance.

*Climber on **Fire in the Hole** (5.10d), Cochise Stronghold, Arizona.* PHOTO BY ERIC J. HÖRST

Given this perspective, view this chapter on nutrition, rest, and injury prevention as the linchpin that binds this book's many aspects into a complete program for achieving stellar results. First, I'll outline the basics of optimal sports nutrition, including a cutting-edge strategy to accelerate recovery after a workout. Next, we'll examine the minimum requirements for rest days and sleep, since it's during these times that you literally grow stronger. Finally, we'll take a look at five rules for avoiding injury due to overuse and overtraining, as both will rob you of the very thing you want—to become better conditioned and climb harder!

Optimal Sports Nutrition

For some readers, the subject of optimal sport nutrition will require a paradigm shift away from the understanding of nutrition learned through gimmicky diet books or the hokum of TV infomercials. Fortunately, optimal sports nutrition is not that complex a subject, and upcoming I will provide a primer on the critical elements. For more information on weight-loss strategies, turn to page 62 in chapter 4; for an in-depth study on this subject, I encourage you to read *Training for Climbing*, which includes a full chapter on performance nutrition.

Carbohydrate

First, let's discard the four-food-groups and three-square-meals-a-day nutritional models that many of us learned in school—these are antiquated concepts and not ideal for a serious athlete. The new model is the Food Guide Pyramid (see figure 12.1), which places more emphasis on fruits, vegetables, bread,

Figure 12.1 Food Guide Pyramid

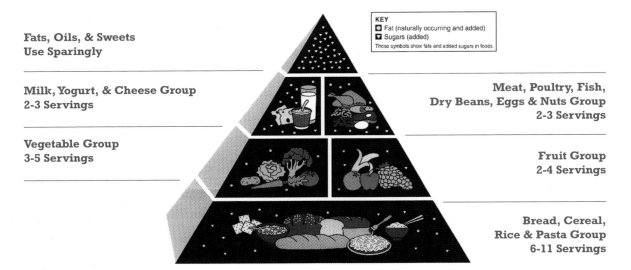

Fats, Oils, & Sweets
Use Sparingly

Milk, Yogurt, & Cheese Group
2-3 Servings

Vegetable Group
3-5 Servings

KEY
☐ Fat (naturally occurring and added)
☑ Sugars (added)
These symbols show fats and added sugars in foods.

Meat, Poultry, Fish,
Dry Beans, Eggs & Nuts Group
2-3 Servings

Fruit Group
2-4 Servings

Bread, Cereal,
Rice & Pasta Group
6-11 Servings

The USDA's Food Guide Pyramid is still the best model for proper eating. The agency has developed a new take on this called **My Pyramid Plan,** *which suggests adjusting the amounts of these foods according to your age, sex, and physical activity. To develop a personalized eating plan, see* **www.mypyramid.gov.** COURTESY OF USDA AND DHHS

rice, pasta, and cereal. These carbohydrate-rich foods form the foundation of the pyramid, as they should of your diet.

Carbohydrate, which is converted to glucose and glycogen in the body, is the ultimate fuel for intense physical exercise such as climbing and training for climbing, so it's best to consume five or six small meals or snacks containing carbohydrate throughout the day. This eating strategy supports steady blood sugar levels, and thus steady energy and mental focus, as well as a constant supply of glycogen to refuel the muscles. Conversely, going too long between meals or eating the wrong foods (more on this in a minute) will lead to spikes and troughs in blood sugar level and corresponding vacillations in energy and mental sharpness. Furthermore, too small of a total number of calories per day from carbohydrates will hinder supercompensation and slow recovery from exercise.

Determining the optimal amount of carbohy-

drate to consume in a day can be difficult, but it is something you can suss out with some experimentation and heightened awareness of your energy levels. A few classic signs that you are consuming too little carbohydrate are unusual tiredness or weakness while training or climbing, strangely weak and tired muscles despite a one- or two-day rest, and poor mental alertness. Use the calorie calculator on page 64 to estimate your daily caloric needs according to your body weight, metabolism, and activity level.

In choosing foods for your snacks and meals, it is important to understand that not all carbohydrate-based foods are created equal. While all forms of carbohydrate contain 4 calories per gram, the rate at which they are digested and transformed to blood glucose varies greatly. As mentioned above, dramatic changes in blood sugar level affect your energy level, mood, and focus, so it's best to consume mainly the type of carbohydrates that elicit only small changes

Table 12.1 Glycemic Index of Common Foods

HIGH (>70)	MEDIUM (50–70)	LOW (< 50)
Sports drinks 70–85	Banana 55	Balance Bar 30
Clif Bar 70+	PowerBar 65	Peanuts 14
Bagel 72	Raisins 64	Apple 38
Carrots 71	Granola bars 61	Orange 43
Corn chips 73	Macaroni 64	Pear 36
Cornflakes 77	Shredded wheat 58	Grapefruit 23
Doughnut 76	Sweet potato 54	Yogurt (with fruit) 30
Honey 73	Bran muffin 60	All-Bran 42
Candies 70–85	Oatmeal 61	Spaghetti 41
Potatoes 83	Cookies 60	Beans 48
Rice (instant) 91	Orange juice 57	Lentils 28
Rice cakes 82	Soft drinks 68	Milk (skim) 32
Glucose 100	Sucrose 65	Fructose 23

in blood sugar. Fortunately, there's the glycemic index (GI) to help you select the right carbohydrate sources (see table 12.1). Foods with a high GI cause a rapid increase in blood sugar and often a subsequent insulin release with the telltale energy trough (and sometimes even sleepiness) that soon follows. Medium- and low-GI foods produce more subtle changes in blood sugar and hence sustain stable energy level, mood, and concentration. Consequently, it is best to consume mainly low- to medium-GI foods during rest days and in the hours leading up to exercise. Only during intense exercise and the two hours following exercise do you want to consume high-GI foods, since the resultant rise in blood sugar level will help sustain fatiguing exercise and best initiate recovery immediately afterward.

Protein

Nearer the top of the Food Pyramid are the protein-rich food groups such as animal and dairy products, beans, and nuts. Since many foods in these groups also possess high amounts of fat, serious athletes tend to avoid them. The result is often insufficient protein intake, which is counterproductive in the quest to build stronger muscles, tendons, and connective tissues. The bottom line: Shortchange yourself on protein and you are shortchanging your muscles and not recovering optimally.

So how much protein does your athlete's body really need? Furthermore, how can you consume enough protein without overdosing on saturated fats? A good estimate of the minimum daily requirement for protein is 1 gram per kilogram of body weight, with a more liberal estimate being 1.5 grams per kilo.

Applying these ratios to my 160-pound (73 kg) body means I should consume between 73 and 110 grams of protein per day. This amount would certainly be fattening and unhealthy if I tried to eat all my protein in the form of red meat and high-fat dairy products. I rarely consume these foods, however, yet I never fail to consume my personal target of 100 grams of protein per day. I can easily reach this goal with four servings of skim milk (a total of 32 grams of protein), several servings of vegetables (5–10 grams), a serving of lean meat or beans (15–25 grams), and a small whey protein shake at breakfast and before bedtime (40 grams of total protein). You could certainly replace the protein shakes or some of the skim milk with yogurt or an extra serving of lean meat and still consume an adequate amount of protein without taking a huge calorie or fat hit. Speaking of fat . . .

Fat

Fats have a bad name among athletes—I admit that I've dissed them more than a few times over the years!—yet not all types of fat are bad. In fact, you may be surprised to learn that you need a steady diet of certain fats to build tissue, lubricate joints, and help combat inflammation, among other things. The problem is that average Americans consume more than 40 percent of their daily calories from fats and oils, and a large portion of these fat calories come from unhealthy nonessential and refined fats.

Note in figure 12.1 that fats and oils form only the tip of the Food Pyramid. Therefore, a climber serious about training and performance must limit fat consumption to just 20 percent of total daily calories (carbohydrate and protein should make up 65 percent and 15 percent of total caloric intake, respectively). Let's run the numbers for an average climber (like me) who weighs about 160 pounds and consumes around 2,500 calories per day. Twenty percent of 2,500 calories is 500 calories, and at 9 calories per gram of fat, I must limit myself to 55 grams of fat per day. This might seem like a lot or a little, depending on your perspective—I have known climbers who swore they'd never eat more than 25 grams of fat per day, while others consume

more than 55 in a single meal at McDonald's! Clearly, neither approach is ideal.

The approach I advocate is to not obsess over fat (in either way), and to let your fat intake "just happen" as you consume your planned, healthy meals throughout the day. Certainly it's advisable to avoid fast foods, fried foods, and all snack foods packaged for maximum shelf life (which surely contain a high amount of dangerous trans fats). However, fats ingested in eating lean meats such as grilled chicken, fish, or a small piece of red meat are mainly good fats, as are most fats contained in nuts, beans, olive-oil-based salad dressing, and many nutrition bars. If these foods are regular staples of your current diet, while the aforementioned fast foods are a rare treat, then you are with the program already!

Water

Whether you are training indoors, climbing outdoors, or just taking a rest day, sustaining proper hydration is essential for optimal performance, injury prevention, and accelerating recovery. Studies have shown that even slight dehydration (a 1 to 3 percent loss of water) results in reduced concentration, enhanced fatigue, and a drop in maximum strength. Furthermore, dehydration makes you more susceptible to cramps, muscle pulls, and even joint and tendon injuries. Clearly, sustaining proper hydration throughout the day is as important as any other aspect of your optimal sports nutrition program.

How much water do you need to consume? Well, this depends on a number of factors including your body weight, your level of activity, and the ambient temperature and humidity. As a rule of thumb, however, it's a good idea to prehydrate one hour before training or climbing by drinking two cups or more of water. Throughout your workout or day of climbing, you want to consume a minimum of one cup (an eight-ounce serving) of water or sports drink every hour. Double or triple this amount in hot weather, as your perspiration rate will be substantially higher.

Vitamins, Sports Drinks, and Other Supplements

Food supplements are ubiquitous these days, with countless sports drinks, vitamins, protein shakes, and other "performance boosting" concoctions and functional foods filling the shelves at health food and grocery stores alike. As a rule, these products—especially the most hyped—provide little benefit and therefore are a colossal waste of money. That said, there are a few products valuable for a serious athlete working to enhance performance and accelerate recovery.

Given the streamlined diet of a serious athlete, I feel it's a wise investment to take a daily multivitamin each morning. Furthermore, research has shown that consuming extra amounts of vitamin C (500 to 1,000 milligrams) and vitamin E (200 to 400 IUs) can enhance the recovery and overall health of a hard-training athlete. Supplemental protein is also a good investment, especially if you consume little meat or dairy. Whey protein powder mixed into a glass of water, juice, or skim milk is the ideal source of extra protein. Drinking a whey protein shake before bedtime and first thing in the morning will provide high-quality protein before and immediately after your six- to nine-hour daily fast (very important!).

Lastly, I'm going to tell you about some exciting research in the area of recovery drinks. While sugar-laced sports drinks have been around since the advent of Gatorade in the 1970s, recent research shows that consuming a sports drink (immediately following a workout) containing both carbohydrate and protein triggers a faster recovery rate than does a conventional carbohydrate-only sports drink. Two popular drink mixes with an effective blend of carbohydrate and protein are Accelerade and PowerBar Recovery Drink. As an alternative to these drinks, you could consume a sugar-based sports drink (like Gatorade) followed by a high-protein drink (such as whey mixed in skim milk). In the case of a hard workout or full day of climbing, you would want to consume about 100 grams of liquid carbohydrate along with 25 grams of liquid protein. Research has shown that you can accelerate recovery by as much as 50 percent if you consume a drink with a four-to-one carbohydrate-to-protein ratio within two hours of completing your workout—the sooner, the better.

Sleep and Recovery Requirements

The act of physical conditioning doesn't make you stronger; it merely stimulates the body's growth mechanisms into motion. It's during periods of rest and sleep that your body actually recovers and supercompensates to a level higher than before the workout. Therefore, your conditioning workouts must be balanced with adequate periods of rest in order to produce the adaptations that will enhance your physical capabilities and climbing performance.

There are two categories of rest to consider: your hours of sleep per night and the number of rest days you take between workouts or days of climbing. In terms of sleep, it's important to recognize that the body repairs itself and new growth occurs primarily during your sleeping hours. Therefore, the amount of sleep you get the night of a hard workout is as important as your use of proper training exercises and consumption of sufficient nutrients. The bare minimum amount of sleep per night is seven to eight hours, with nine hours being optimal after an especially hard day of climbing. If you are like most people, that kind of free time is hard to come by, but you might be able to pull it off by giving up some nighttime activities (TV and such) in favor of going to bed earlier. Remind yourself that sleep is an essential part of your conditioning program. What are your priorities?

Specifying the optimal number of rest days between workouts or days of climbing is harder to pin down. There are many factors that contribute to rate of recovery, such as the quality of your diet, hours of sleep, rest-day activity, level of fitness, age, and genetics. Another major factor is workout intensity. Complete recovery from a low-intensity stamina workout such as moderate climbing or jogging may take just twenty-four hours, whereas recovery from a power-training session or two-hour anaerobic-endurance workout could take as much as three to five days. Ultimately, you need to be aware of your body's signals and continue with your next workout only when you feel fully recovered.

If you ever sense that you are getting weaker, despite your dedicated efforts in the gym, there's a good chance that your workout-to-rest ratio needs adjustment. Overtraining is an epidemic among enthusiastic climbers, and it's a leading cause of frustrating performance plateaus and injury. If you frequently arrive at the gym or crags feeling tired and unmotivated, or if you feel weak and out of whack on the rock, then you may be suffering from overtraining. Although you may get away with this for a while, the practice of constantly climbing weak and tired will eventually lead to overtraining, a decline in performance, and perhaps injury or illness.

The antidote to overtraining is over-resting! Begin by taking three to seven days off from conditioning and climbing activities. After this break you should return to a schedule of regular exercise—but at a frequency reduced by one day per week. For example, if you previously climbed and trained a total of four days per week, reduce this to three. Increasing your quantity of rest will begin a new growth phase with corresponding gains in conditioning and climbing performance!

Injury Prevention Tips

In concluding this text on conditioning for climbers, I will provide you with five tips for reducing your injury risk and hopefully remaining on-route to reaching your climbing goals. The recent escalation in chronic injuries of the fingers, elbows, and shoulders is frightening, so the wise climber will be proactive in mitigating injury risk. Remind yourself frequently that an injury is the single greatest barrier between you and your conditioning and climbing goals. Here's what you can do to prevent this.

Limit Climbing and Training to Four Days a Week—or Less

As a rule it is counterproductive to climb and train more than four days per week, in aggregate. For example, if you are climbing four days a week on the rock, in the gym, or a combination, you should do no other sport-specific training during the three remaining days of the week. Even with three days' rest out of seven, your body will struggle to repair the microtraumas incurred to the tendons and muscles during your four climbing days. For this reason, it is wise to utilize a training cycle that provides a complete week off every two or three months.

If you are engaging in an elite-level conditioning program, you may even need to limit yourself to just three climbing/exercise days per week. In this case, you might be climbing and training for climbing on a Tuesday, Thursday, and Saturday schedule. Of the remaining four nonclimbing days, you could engage in aerobic activity and antagonist conditioning, but absolutely no pull-muscle or climbing-related exercise. Limiting yourself in this way can be very difficult—especially if you possess a home wall or gym membership—but you must leverage your training knowledge and desire to achieve uncommon results and stay with the program! Of course, many folks just can't do this, and they are destined to become one of the walking wounded.

Don't Skip the Warm-Up and Cool-Down

I'm always surprised by the number of climbers I observe who arrive at the gym or crag and just start climbing without any warm-up activity whatsoever. No serious athlete in any other sport would ever consider jumping into full-speed training or competition without warming up, yet many climbers do. This probably has to do with the fact that, unlike participants in other sports, most climbers don't have a coach to direct warm-up drills and workout strategy. As a self-directed, self-coached activity, climbing necessitates that you play the roles of both coach and athlete—you must compel yourself to do the right things right. That's the essence of an effective conditioning program.

All you need by way of a good warm-up is to break a light sweat for five to fifteen minutes by jogging, hiking, or riding, or at the very least climbing around on large holds and easy terrain to elevate your heart rate. This then prepares you to engage in some of the stretching exercises described in chapter 3, after which you are ready to start climbing on a series of progressively more difficult boulder problems or roped climbs. The entire warm-up process will take anywhere from fifteen to thirty minutes,

but it will leave you ready to execute your most difficult exercises or project climb with the least risk of incurring an injury.

A brief cool-down is also beneficial to loosen up tight muscle groups and enhance the recovery process. In particular, stretching and a few minutes of light aerobic activity will sustain elevated blood flow to the muscles and thus speed dispersion of lactic acid accumulated in the most fatigued muscles.

Regularly Train the Antagonist Muscles

As explained in chapter 8, training the antagonist muscles is one of the most overlooked—and vital—parts of the conditioning program. Muscle imbalances in the forearms, shoulders, and torso are primary factors in many of the overuse injuries experienced by climbers. If you are serious about climbing your best and preventing injury, then you must commit to training the antagonist muscles twice per week.

The time investment is minimal—about twenty minutes, twice a week, is all you need to tone and strengthen the various opposing muscle groups. I prefer doing these exercises on my rest days between climbing workouts, although you could also engage in this push-muscle training at the end of your climbing session. Either way, I advise doing all of the antagonist exercises described in this book, as well as a few of the core-conditioning exercises detailed in chapter 5.

Leverage Periodization

In chapter 1 you learned about the principle of variation and how a periodization scheme will supercharge your conditioning program. As explained, periodization involves a premeditated variation in workout focus, intensity, and volume, which in the long term produces a maximal training response. Periodization also reduces the risk of overuse injury

Indoor climbing will make you stronger but you still run the risk of injury. Limit climbing and sport-specific training to a total of four days per week.

PHOTO BY ERIC J. HÖRST

since the training focus and intensity change every few days or weeks.

In a highly stressful sport such as climbing, the most valuable aspect of periodization may be the intermittent rest phases or breaks away from all sport-specific activity. Chapter 10 promoted use of a training cycle such as the 4-3-2-1 Cycle for most intermediate and elite climbers. This training cycle provides one full week of rest out of every ten-week cycle for systemic recovery and to blunt long-term accumulation of overuse stress. In the yearlong macrocycle, it is similarly advisable to take an entire month off from climbing-related stresses. These breaks away from climbing go a long way toward allowing the slow-to-adapt tendons and ligaments to catch up with the more quickly occurring gains in muscular strength. Be wise—periodize!

Strive for Optimal Rest and Nutrition

This final tip completes the circle of knowledge for this final chapter of *Conditioning for Climbers*, since it underscores the importance of proper rest and nutrition. I encourage you to reread the section on optimal sports nutrition on page 181, and then internalize and apply this information. No matter your age or ability, improving your nutrition and recovery habits is essential to reaching your conditioning and climbing goals.

Since you have now read this book to its end, it's clear that you are a climber passionate about reaching your true potential. This book has covered the many facets of conditioning for climbing that must be interlaced to form a superlative and uncommonly effective program. Remember that the chapters relating to self-assessment, warm-up, and recovery are as important as those dealing with developing greater strength, power, and stamina conditioning. Becoming the best climber you can be takes many years of dedicated, comprehensive effort, and I hope this book will be your constant companion on this wonderful adventure.

Be safe, be strong, and always have fun whether you are climbing or conditioning for climbing!

Appendix A: Muscle Anatomy

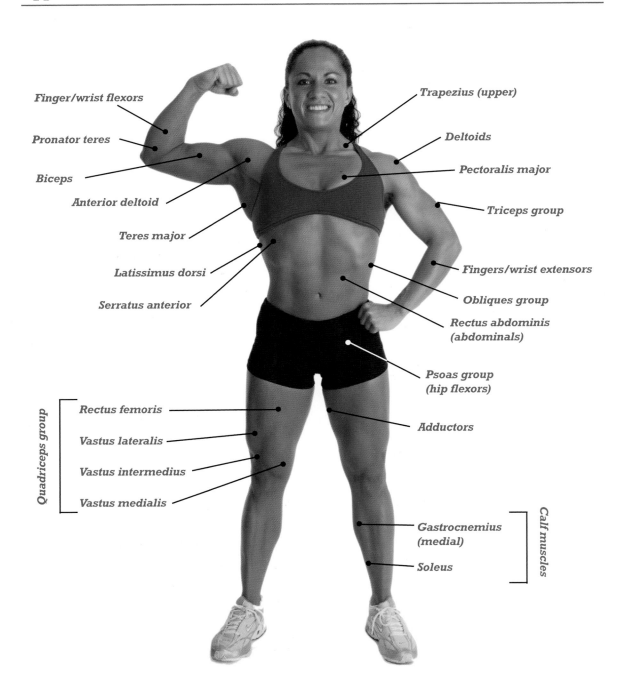

Finger/wrist flexors

Pronator teres

Biceps

Anterior deltoid

Teres major

Latissimus dorsi

Serratus anterior

Trapezius (upper)

Deltoids

Pectoralis major

Triceps group

Fingers/wrist extensors

Obliques group

Rectus abdominis
(abdominals)

Psoas group
(hip flexors)

Adductors

Quadriceps group

Rectus femoris

Vastus lateralis

Vastus intermedius

Vastus medialis

Gastrocnemius
(medial)

Soleus

Calf muscles

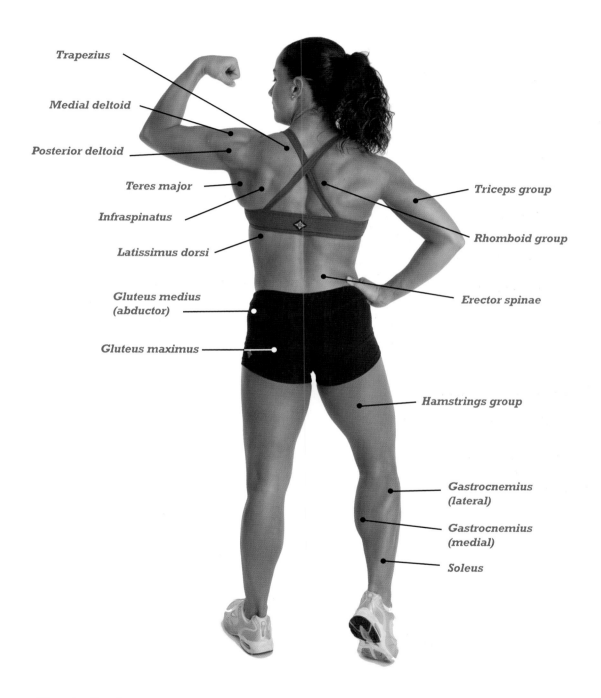

Trapezius

Medial deltoid

Posterior deltoid

Teres major

Infraspinatus

Latissimus dorsi

**Gluteus medius
(abductor)**

Gluteus maximus

Triceps group

Rhomboid group

Erector spinae

Hamstrings group

**Gastrocnemius
(lateral)**

**Gastrocnemius
(medial)**

Soleus

Appendix B: Training and Climbing Macrocycle Chart

Name/Year												
				Training Objectives and Seasonal Climbing Goals								
Month	Jan	Feb	Mar	Apr	May	Jun	Jul	Aug	Sep	Oct	Nov	Dec
Week	1 2 3 4 5	6 7 8 9	10 11 12 13	14 15 16 17 18	19 20 21 22	23 24 25 26	27 28 29 30 31	32 33 34 35 36	37 38 39	40 41 42 43	44 45 46 47	48 49 50 51 52
Training Focus — Climbing/stamina / Max. strength and power / Anaerobic endurance / Rest												
Total number of days per week of finger training or climbing — 7 6 5 4 3 2 1												
Benchmark achievements and notes												

Glossary

The following is a compilation of some of the technical terms and climbing jargon used throughout this book.

active recovery—Restoration of homeostasis following vigorous exercise that involves continued light-intensity movement; facilitates faster recovery by enhancing lactate removal from the blood.

acute—Having rapid onset and severe symptoms.

adaptive response—Physiological changes in structure or function particularly related to response to a training overload.

aerobic—Any physical activity deriving energy from the breakdown of glycogen in the presence of oxygen, thus producing little or no lactic acid, enabling an athlete to continue exercise much longer.

agonist—A muscle directly engaged in a muscular contraction.

anaerobic—Energy production in the muscles involving the breakdown of glycogen in the absence of oxygen; a by called lactic acid is formed, resulting in rapid fatigue and cessation of physical activity.

anaerobic endurance—The ability to continue moderate- to high-intensity activity over a period of time; commonly called power endurance or power stamina by climbers, though these terms are scientifically incorrect.

anaerobic threshold—The workload or level of oxygen consumption where lactate production by the working muscles exceeds the rate of lactate removal by the liver. Typically this occurs at 50 to 80 percent of maximum intensity of exercise, and in proportion to your level of anaerobic-endurance conditioning.

antagonist—A muscle providing an opposing force to the primary (agonist) muscles in action.

atrophy—Gradual shrinking and deconditioning of muscle tissue from disuse.

basal metabolic rate—The minimum level of energy required to sustain the body's vital functions.

campus (or campusing)—Climbing an overhanging section of rock or artificial wall with no feet, usually in a dynamic left hand, right hand, left hand (et cetera) sequence.

campus training—A sport-specific form of plyometric exercise developed by Wolfgang Güllich at the Campus Center (a weight-lifting facility at the University of Nuremberg, Germany).

capillary—The tiny blood vessels that receive blood flow from the arteries, interchange substances between the blood and the tissues, and return the blood to the veins.

capillary density—Number of capillaries per unit area of muscle tissue. Capillary density increases, mainly in slow-twitch fibers, in response to aerobic training.

chronic—Continuing over time.

concentric contraction—Any movement involving a shortening of muscles fibers while developing tension, as in the biceps muscle during a pull-up.

contact strength—Initial grip strength upon touching a handhold.

crimp grip—The most natural (and stressful) way to grip a rock hold, characterized by hyperextension of the first joint in the fingers and nearly full flexion of the second joint.

detraining—Reversal of positive adaptations to chronic exercise upon cessation of an exercise program.

dynamic move—An explosive leap for a hold otherwise out of reach.

dyno—Short for "dynamic."

eccentric contraction—Muscle action in which the muscle resists as it is forced to lengthen, as in the biceps during the lowering phase of a pull-up.

endurance—Ability to perform physical work for an extended period of time. Cardiovascular endurance (also called stamina) is directly related to VO_2 max, whereas muscular endurance is influenced by circulation and oxygen availability.

epicondylitis—Inflammation of the tendon origins of the forearm flexors (medial) or extensors (lateral) near the elbow.

ergogenic—Performance enhancing.

extension—A movement that takes the two ends of a jointed body part away from each other, as in straightening the arm.

flash pump—A rapid, often vicious, muscular pump resulting from strenuous training or climbing without first performing a proper (gradual) warm-up.

flexion—A movement that brings the ends of a body part closer together, as in bending the arm.

fingerboard or hangboard—a training apparatus, commonly found in climbing gyms or installed above a doorway at a climber's residence, that facilitates climbing-specific finger and arm training (pull-ups, finger hangs, and such).

glycogen—Compound chains of glucose stored in the muscle and liver for use during aerobic or anaerobic exercise.

glycemic index (GI)—A scale that classifies how the ingestion of various foods affects blood sugar levels in comparison with the ingestion of straight glucose.

homeostasis—The body's tendency to maintain a steady state despite external changes.

honed—In extremely good shape; with low body fat.

hormone—A chemical secreted into the bloodstream to regulate the function of a certain organ.

Hypergravity Isolation Training (HIT)—A highly refined and specific method of training maximum finger strength and upper-body power by climbing on identical finger holds (isolation) with greater than body weight (hypergravity). Also known as Hörst Isolation Training.

hypergravity training—A highly effective method of training maximum strength that involves climbing or training with weight added to the body (simulates hypergravity).

hypertrophy—Enlargement in size, as in muscular hypertrophy.

insulin—A hormone that decreases blood glucose level by driving glucose from the blood into muscle and fat cells.

interval training—A method of anaerobic endurance training that involves brief periods of intense training interspaced with periods of rest or low-intensity training.

isometric—Muscular contraction resulting in no shortening of the muscle (no movement).

kinesthetic—The sense derived from muscular contractions and limb movements.

lactic acid—An acid by-product of the anaerobic metabolism of glucose during intense muscular exercise.

lactic acid system—Energy pathway used in high-intensity activity over a short duration.

ligament—Fibrous, connective tissue that connects bone to bone, or bone to cartilage, to hold together and support the joints.

lunge—An out-of-control dynamic move; an explosive jump for a far-off hold.

macronutrients—Basic nutrients (carbohydrates, fat, and protein) needed for energy, cell growth, and organ function.

maximum strength—The peak force of a muscular contraction, irrespective of the time element. Also called limit strength.

micronutrients—Noncaloric nutrients needed in very small amounts, as in vitamins and minerals.

motor learning—The set of internal processes associated with practice or experience leading to a relatively permanent gain in performance capability.

motor skill—A skill where the primary determinant of success is the movement component itself.

open-hand grip—The less stressful finger grip involving only slight flexion of the finger joints.

overhanging—A wall surface that angles outward beyond vertical, so that the top of the wall overhangs its base.

overload—Subjecting a part of the body to greater efforts (intensity or volume) than it is accustomed to in order to elicit a training response.

overtraining—Constant severe training that does not provide adequate time for recovery; symptoms include increased frequency of injury, decreased performance, irritability, and apathy.

overuse—Excessive repeated exertion or shock that results in injuries such as inflammation of the muscles and tendons.

plyometric—An exercise that suddenly preloads and forces the stretching of a muscle an instant prior to its concentric contraction, as in dynamic up-and-down campus training.

power—A measure of both force and speed (speed = distance x time) of a muscular contraction through a given range of motion. Power is the explosive aspect of strength.

pronation—The inward turning of a body part, as in turning the forearm inward and the palm facedown.

proprioceptive neuromuscular facilitation (PNF)—A stretching technique that couples contraction and relaxation to enhance stretching gains. Most commonly, a five- to ten-second muscle contraction (against resistance from a partner) is followed by a relaxation period during which the partner slowly applies pressure to increase the range of the stretch.

pumped—When the muscles become engorged with blood due to extended physical exertion.

recruitment—Systematic increase in the number of active motor units called upon during muscular contraction.

schema—A set of rules, usually developed and applied unconsciously by the motor system in the brain and spinal cord, relating how to move and adjust muscle forces, body positions, and so on given the parameters at hand, such as steepness of the rock, friction qualities, holds being used, and type of terrain.

send—Short for "ascend."

skill—A capability to bring about an end result with maximum certainty, minimum energy, and minimum time.

slow-twitch fibers—Muscle fiber type that contracts slowly and is used most in moderate-intensity endurance activities, such as easy to moderate climbing or running.

sport climbing—Usually refers to any indoor or outdoor climbing on bolt-protected routes.

spotter—A training partner who assists you in executing an exercise safely and effectively. Also, a person designated to slow the fall of a boulderer, with the main goal of keeping the boulderer's head from hitting the ground.

stabilizer muscle—A muscle that is stimulated to help anchor or stabilize the position of a bone.

strength—The amount of muscle force that can be exerted; speed and distance are not factors of strength.

supercompensate—The body's recovery process of adaptation and overcompensation to the stress of exercise.

supination—Rotation of the forearm outward and palm upward.

synovial fluid—A viscid fluid secreted by the membrane lining joints, tendon sheaths, and bursae to lubricate and cushion them during movement.

Tabata—A grueling interval-training protocol involving twenty seconds of maximum-intensity exercise followed by ten seconds of rest; usually repeated up to eight times. Named after its developer, Izumi Tabata.

tendinitis—A disorder involving the inflammation of a tendon and synovial membrane at a joint.

tendinosis—Chronic tendon pain due to an accumulation of microscopic injuries that don't heal properly; the main problem, then, is failed healing, not inflammation.

tendon—A white fibrous cord of dense connective tissue that attaches muscle to bone.

training effect—A basic principle of exercise science. It states that adaptation occurs from an exercise only in those parts or systems of the body that are stressed by the exercise.

toprope—The most secure roped climbing setup in which the rope passes through an anchor atop the route.

vein—A vessel that returns blood from the various parts of the body to the heart.

visualization—Controlled and directed imagery that can be used for awareness building, monitoring and self-regulation, healing, and, most important, mental programming for good performances.

VO$_2$ max—Maximal oxygen uptake, as in the measurement of maximum aerobic power.

wired—Known well, as in a wired route.

working—Practicing the moves on a difficult route via toprope or hangdogging.

Suggested Reading

Burke, Edmund. *Optimal Muscle Recovery.* Garden City Park, N.Y.: Avery Publishing Group, 1999.

Goddard, Dale. *Performance Rock Climbing.* Mechanicsburg, Pa.: Stackpole, 1993.

Guten, Gary. *Injuries in Outdoor Recreation.* Guilford, Conn.: The Globe Pequot Press/FalconGuides, 2005.

Hochholzer, Thomas, et al. *One Move Too Many.* Ebenhausen, Germany: Lochner-Verlag, 2003.

Hörst, Eric J. *Training for Climbing.* Guilford, Conn.: The Globe Pequot Press/FalconGuides, 2003.

Hurni, Michelle. *Coaching Climbing.* Guilford, Conn.: The Globe Pequot Press/FalconGuides, 2003.

Stricker, Lauri. *Pilates for the Outdoor Athlete.* Conifer, Colo.: Fulcrum, 2007.

Index

quadriceps and hip flexors, 47
lunging, one-arm, 96

M

macrocycle
    sample, 167
    blank, 192
maximum strength, 4
mental skills, 6–7
    over-fifty climbers, 179
    self-assessment, 16
microcycles, sample
    advanced climbers, 172
    beginner climbers, 160
    big-wall climbers, 172
    intermediate climbers, 165
multiday climbing, 152–54
multipitch climbing
    conditioning for, 169–71
    sample workout, 170
    stamina conditioning for, 148–52

N

neck circles, 30
nutrition, 181–86
    carbohydrates, 63, 64, 181–83
    fat, 63, 64, 184
    injury prevention and, 189
    protein, 63, 64, 183–84
    self-assessment, 20
    surveillance of, 63–64
    vitamins, sports drinks, and other
        supplements, 186
    water, 184

O

oblique crunches, 71
obliques
    conditioning, 68–72
    stretch, 50
one-arm, one-leg bridge, 80
one-arm lock-off, 113

one-arm lunging, 96
one-arm traversing, 95
order of exercise, 10
over-fifty climbers, 177–79
    injury avoidance, 177–79
    physical conditioning, 179
    technical and mental mastery, 179
    tips, 177
overload, 9

P

periodization, 10–11, 189
physical demands of climbing, 4, 6
    over-fifty climbers, 179
Physioball exercises, 76–79
piriformis stretch, 43
power
    defined, 117
    physical demands of climbing, 4
power training
    4-3-2-1 Training Cycle, 162
    upper-body, 117–23
pronators, 134–35
protein, 63, 64, 183–84
pull-downs, heavy, 110
pull-muscle conditioning, 164
pull-ups
    aided, 57
    basic, 56
    intervals, 123
    power, 117
    uneven-grip, 112
    weighted, 110
push-ups, 58
pyramid training, fingerboard, 104

Q

quadricep stretch, 46, 47

R

recovery, 11, 186–87
reps, optimal, 10

rest
> 4-3-2-1 Training Cycle, 163
> injury prevention and, 189
> requirements for, 186–87

reverse wrist curls, 132–33

rhomboid stretch, 36

rope climbing, 122–23

rotator cuff, 142–45
> external rotation, 144–45
> internal rotation, 142–43
> overview, 142

route intervals, 148, 151

running intervals, 151–52

S

self-assessment, 13–22
> climbing experience, 14
> general conditioning level, 17
> injury risk, 19
> lifestyle and discipline, 21
> mental skills, 16
> nutritional habits, 20
> overview, 13
> sport-specific conditioning, 18
> technical skills, 15

sets, optimal, 10

shoulder press, 136–37

shoulder shrugs, 29, 141

shrugs, 29, 141

side hip raises, 72

side squat, 60

sleep, 186

snowflake principle, 9

specificity principle, 9

sport climbing
> conditioning for, 168–69
> stamina conditioning for, 148–52
> workout, sample, 169

sports drinks, 186

sport-specific conditioning, 7, 9
> self-assessment, 18

squat, side, 60

stamina conditioning, 147–54
> all- and multiday climbing, 152–54
> bouldering, sport climbing, and multipitch routes,
> 148–52
> 4-3-2-1 Training Cycle, 162
> overview, 6, 147–48

steep-wall lock-offs, 125–27

steep-wall traversing, 82

strength training
> finger conditioning, 85–102
> 4-3-2-1 Training Cycle, 162
> strength types, 4
> upper-body, 109–15

stretching
> beginner climbers, 158
> intermediate climbers, 162
> lower-body, 41–49
> tips, 40
> torso/core, 50–53
> upper-body, 33–39

Superhero exercise, 74

supplements, food, 186

Swiss ball exercises, 76–79

System Wall, 105–6

T

Tabata Protocol, 106

taping to reinforce tendons, 98

technical skills, 6–7
> over-fifty climbers, 179
> self-assessment, 15

tendons, taping to reinforce, 98

torso/core stretches, 50–53
> abdominals, 51
> lower back and hips, 53
> obliques, 50
> overview, 50
> trunk rotation, 52

training cycles, 162–63

trapezius stretch, 36

About the Author

An accomplished climber of more than thirty years, Eric J. Hörst (pronounced *Hurst*) has climbed extensively across the United States and has established more than 450 first ascents. A student and teacher of climbing performance, Eric has personally helped train hundreds of climbers, and his training books and concepts have spread to climbers in more than fifty countries. He is widely recognized for his innovative practice methods and training techniques, and since 1994 he has served as a training products design consultant and online Training Center editor for Nicros, Inc., a leading manufacturer of climbing walls and handholds.

Eric is author of *Training for Climbing, How to Climb 5.12,* and *Learning to Climb Indoors.* He regularly contributes to outdoor and fitness magazines such as *Climbing, Rock & Ice, Urban Climber, Outside, National Geographic Adventure, Men's Health, Muscle & Fitness, Experience Life,* and *Men's Journal,* and he has appeared on numerous TV broadcasts. Eric maintains a climbing performance blog for Mountain-Zone.com and broadcasts monthly Training Tip podcasts at PodClimber.com. Visit Eric's website, TrainingForClimbing.com, for training articles and information on all his books, or to schedule a training seminar, an editorial interview, or a speaking engagement.

Eric currently lives in Lancaster, Pennsylvania, with his wife, Lisa Ann, and his sons, Cameron and Jonathan.

PHOTO BY ERIC McCALLISTER

Other Books by Eric J. Hörst

Training for Climbing (FalconGuides, 2003) is a comprehensive, science-based tome that presents a unique synthesis of leading-edge strength training, tried-and-true practice strategies, and powerful mental-training techniques that will empower you to climb better, regardless of your current ability. *TFC* is the ultimate resource on all aspects of climbing performance, and it's the training text of choice as used by climbers around the world!

How to Climb 5.12 (FalconGuides, 2003) is a performance guidebook to attaining the most rapid gains in climbing ability possible. It provides streamlined instruction on vital topics such as accelerating learning of skills, training the mind and body, and becoming an effective on-sight and redpoint climber.

Learning to Climb Indoors (FalconGuides, 2006) is the most complete book available on indoor climbing. Topics covered include beginning and advanced climbing techniques, tactics, strategy, basic gear, safety techniques, self-assessment, and a primer on mental training and physical conditioning. This guide includes everything you need to know from day one as a climber through your first year or two in the sport.